The soul of Chaplin's Little Tramp is mimicked in the spring of his cane.

SIR CH

CHAPLIN, THE FUNNI

ARLIE

Man in the World

SID FLEISCHMAN

GREENWILLOW BOOKS
An Imprint of HarperCollinsPublishers

The publisher and author gratefully acknowledge
the assistance of the Chaplin estate.

The text of this book is set in Centaur.
Book design by Chad W. Beckerman and Christy Hale

Library of Congress Cataloguing-in-Publication Data
Fleischman, Sid, (date).
Sir Charlie: Chaplin, the funniest man in the
world / by Sid Fleischman.
p. cm.
"Greenwillow Books."
ISBN 978-0-06-189640-8 (trade bdg.)
ISBN 978-0-06-189641-5 (lib. bdg.)
1. Chaplin, Charlie, 1889–1977—Juvenile literature.
2. Comedians—United States—Biography—Juvenile literature.
3. Motion picture actors and actresses—United States—Biography—
Juvenile literature. I. Title.
PN2287.C5F56 2010   791.43'028'0924—dc22[B]   2009019689

10 11 12 13 14 SCP 10 9 8 7 6 5 4 3 2 1
First Edition

 GREENWILLOW BOOKS

HORRORS! A PREFACE!

Choosing a subject for a biography may be as perilous or as charmed as a marriage. A writer chooses with fingers crossed.

In one of his funniest films, a comic epic of war, Charlie Chaplin single-handedly captured thirteen enemy soldiers. When asked how he did it, he famously answered, "I surrounded them."

I surrounded Chaplin to make him the subject of this biography. His rags-to-riches story was, in two words, tragic and wonderful. And it was fun to write.

I grew up laughing at his absurd walk, the amiable tipping of his bowler hat, and the comic skids on one foot as he turned corners.

When I arrived in Hollywood in the mid-1950s to write

screenplays, Chaplin had left town shortly before to take up residence in Switzerland. But his footprints were everywhere.

His old films tutored me. I don't know how many times I had my hero duck a blow, only to have a bystander take the punch. Pure Chaplin.

He made me acutely aware of the bewitchment of comic bits of business. Shuffling cards with the speed of a machine gun. Accidentally stepping into a spittoon. More importantly, he armed my screenplays with the muscle power of pantomime, of pure spectator theater.

That gift of the visual has stayed with me throughout my years as a screenwriter, a novelist, and now, as a biographer.

Thanks, Charlie.

—Sid Fleischman

Santa Monica, California

CONTENTS

Introduction, or
LADIES WILL PLEASE REMOVE THEIR HATS

A DARK-EYED MAN CAME SWAYING DOWN THE street like a tightrope walker. You couldn't miss his yellow checked suit or the angle of his bowler hat, as insolent as a cannonball.

He was an actor and ballad singer in long-ago London, and he had abandoned his wife and two young sons. In past years, not a penny for rent or beefsteaks had he tossed back over his shoulder.

He forged two achievements in life. First, he would drink himself to death by the age of thirty-seven. Second, he would father a genius.

Around the corner, in the evening shadows, often stood an under-sized kid as bony as a bicycle. This night he might be selling boats he'd learned to fold out of newspapers. Abandoned by his actor father, he was doomed to hunger and poverty with a young mother slipping in and out of insanity.

His name was Charles.

Like Houdini freeing himself from a straitjacket, he escaped his ordained captivity in the London slums. When his talents came of age, he began picking through theatrical props. With the sorcery of a Dr. Frankenstein, he assembled another human being. He chose a pair of big, patched shoes and pants large enough to fit a baby elephant. A bowler hat? Yes, of course! And why not a bamboo cane for a touch of elegance?

His creature needed a distinctive walk. Growing up, he'd been a keen observer of Cockney life around him along the docks and roads of Kennington. "Sore feet are always funny—other people's," he said, recalling a quaint old groom tending a public house "who habitually had sore feet . . . from whom I learned to walk."

He had no similar affection for the low Cockney accent and slum argot he'd picked up on the streets of his childhood, though the comforting sound of the Bow bells from a church in Cheapside never entirely dimmed in his ears.

He hitched up his shoulders and tried this stroll and that shuffle. It was only when he turned his feet outward so that each angled off like opposite hands of a clock, at ten past ten, that the shambling walk strolled him into immortality.

He glued on a postage stamp of a black mustache and voilà! The Little Tramp was born.

The alter ego transformed Charlie into the most famous comedian and movie star of his century. He kept the world in stitches. Still does. His audience is eternal, captivated by "that whirling gust of joy" on TV, on tapes and DVDs. Impersonators shuffle along the sidewalks of Hollywood Boulevard to amuse the tourists. Actors imitate him. Look-alike contests were common. Once, during a competition at Grauman's Chinese Theatre in Hollywood, so many mimics flocked in that Charlie, in full makeup, came in third.

With his gift for mimicry, the slum kid from Cockney London forged a social passport into a world of castles and caviar. He became as rich as a king but a whole lot funnier. He struck up friendships with Albert Einstein, with the American poet Carl Sandburg, and with Lord Mountbatten. He could drop so many names he should have been cited for littering.

His name was Chaplin. Charlie Chaplin.

He had absorbed the art of impersonation from his mother. A dancer and singer with a lovely but fragile voice, she taught him to sing and dance a jig for friends as soon as he was off his knees. He was a natural. He easily mimicked her mimicking the theater stars of the day.

In performance one night, she lost her voice in mid-song, blaring forth like a steamboat. The rough, bumptious audience broke into catcalls and roaring boos. In a panic to divert the paying customers from tearing up the seats, the theater manager shoved Charlie onto the stage and told him to sing.

An obedient child, Charlie did what he was told. Blinded by the footlights, he belted out a patter song and did impressions—including one of his mother losing her voice. Coins bounced onto the stage like hail. The curly-haired Cockney kid with the wistful eyes was a hit—a theatrical nova soon to explode before the world.

He was five years old.

Said he, "That night was my first appearance on the stage and Mother's last."

Years would pass before Charlie again stopped the show. At seventeen, he would be a huge hit playing a wobbly drunk on the stage. Tutoring the part by example had been the only gift bestowed by his late father. Before long, the young Charlie took a lease on California sunshine. He became the brightest Hollywood star, ablaze in movie astronomy, and by common consent, "the funniest man in the world."

The ancient Greek mask of comedy now bore the face of a courteous, plucky tramp with a black mustache and a bowler hat. The world was his oyster, but to Charlie's dignified little tramp, oysters always seemed to be out of season.

Chaplin got his laughs without uttering a word. Not a one-liner. Not a quip.

While movies had been invented toward the end of the nineteenth century, they had not yet found their vocal cords. Actors on the screen could declaim to the roofs, but the theaters remained almost as silent as tombs—except for a piano in the dark, playing to the action. Or here and there the crackling of peanuts being freed from their shells by a hungry audience.

The dumb show was no hurdle for Charlie Chaplin. Coming from the knockabout stage, he was already a master of pantomime and physical comedy. He could convey more with a twitch of his absurd little mustache than other actors could with dialogue by the yard.

Since his humor was not verbal but created for the eye, one needed to see what mischief the comic was up to on the screen. Since women wore hats as large as stork nests, if you were seated behind one, you had to bob your head around to view the screen.

Managers were obliged to project messages before the show began.

LADIES WILL PLEASE REMOVE THEIR HATS

In these pages, the view of Charlie Chaplin will be unobstructed.

Chapter One
THE BOY IN THE BLUE VELVET SUIT

IN THE PESKY RAIN ON A MARCH NIGHT IN 1978, nitwit thieves huddled at the grave of Sir Charlie Chaplin and dug up the body of the world-famous comedian. They held it for ransom.

The scheme could have passed as the hectic plot in one of the great filmmaker's comedies of errors.

It was the last fanfare heard around the world in a life that began in 1889 without disturbing a dozing world. London failed to notice and record the arrival of Charles Spencer Chaplin on the evening of April 16. A flu epidemic was tapering off, but the infant was doing fine. Stout Queen Victoria sat on the English throne, but Charles Spencer Chaplin was equally unaware of her.

The parents were music-hall performers; that is to say,

vaudevillians, small fry of the theater in a mad pursuit of fame and fortune. World success would have to cool its heels until the infant grew up and took over the family curse.

The vaudevillians had been wedded for four years when Charlie came along. By then, the marriage had developed dry rot. The senior Charles didn't hang around to do diapers. He packed his ballads and an extra pair of socks and closed the show.

Charlie's mother bravely hung on alone. A Protestant Irish cobbler's daughter named Hannah Hill, she was earning enough money singing Gilbert and Sullivan and lesser patter to care for her two sons. Two?

Before marrying, she had been a woman of some worldly experience. At eighteen she had abandoned modesty to run off to South Africa with a mysterious and moneyed older gentleman. He was whispered to be a Jewish gambler named Sidney Hawkes. She returned to London without a marriage license, without riches, but prodigiously pregnant. Her new husband, Charles Chaplin, charitably adopted the fourteen-week-old boy, Sydney, and promptly began to drink heavily.

A songwriter as well as a performer, the young father enjoyed a prosperous clink of coins in his pocket. With a modest whiskey-barrel

Chaplin's young mother, Hannah, a few years before Charlie was born.

chest, he exhaled both fumes and a light baritone voice that took him to New York. In years hence, the junior Charles, abandoned from early childhood, would take the place by storm, but the senior Chaplin was barely able to raise a drizzle. He returned to England and his favorite pub.

The years of Charlie's earliest, gaslit childhood in Kennington, a decaying borough of London, once the home of the great poet Chaucer, were happy.

Charlie was able to bring forth a few Kennington scenes like yellowed snapshots. He recalled a roomy apartment across the river from the Houses of Parliament. A housemaid. There was almost always a pose of his adored and irrepressible mother, whose long hair, he wrote, "she could sit upon."

His father, the actor, would skip dinner and swallow six raw eggs in port wine to sustain him through his evening stage performance.

Charlie attempted, at age three and a half years, to be the world's youngest magician. Sydney had dazzled him by appearing to swallow a coin, only to reproduce it out of the back of his head. Ever the mimic, Charlie grabbed the coin and swallowed it. Alas, the copper got caught in his throat. A doctor was summoned, who evidently held the boy upside down until the money popped free. Later, as a filmmaker, had Charlie needed the scene, no doubt a jackpot of coins would have come flying out. He learned early that exaggeration did the heavy lifting for comedy.

To enable his mother to sleep late after a theater performance, he recalled surprise pieces of Neapolitan cake to keep him and Sydney happy and quiet when they got out of bed in the morning. He remembered sitting beside her on the roof of a horse-drawn bus and reaching for the leaves of lilac trees in the spring. And there was the blue velvet suit his mother dressed him in, with matching blue gloves. "I was hardly aware of a father," he was to write.

But a housemaid? Could Hannah have afforded such airs? Enter, stage left, another actor and songwriter, dashing Leo Dryden. She bore him a son before he bounced away, taking the lad with him to grow up out of sight, possibly in Canada.

Evidently with some embarrassment, Chaplin airbrushed the Dryden invader out of his autobiography. He would not be the first famous man to run for cover from a blushing past.

Hannah held on to her own two boys. And then, one by one, the lights on her life were snuffed out.

With her voice failing, Hannah's theatrical bookings crashed. Her income vanished. Lily Harley, her stage name, became yesterday's newspaper.

To keep afloat, she sold off her jewelry and everything she owned. Her apartments would shrink to a squalid basement room behind a pickle factory and next to a slaughterhouse.

Barely able to read, Charlie dreamily escaped by struggling through the pages of *Treasure Island*, while he himself lived much like an abandoned waif in a Charles Dickens novel of the London streets.

Chapter Two
BLEAK HOUSES

WALKING AGAINST THE WIND, CHARLIE carried a chair on his back, a pillow, a blanket, and some clothes. The three Chaplins were moving again, as they did every month or so when his mother couldn't pay the rent. The family lived from crisis to crisis, drawn deeper and deeper into poverty.

All that was left of Hannah Chaplin's old life was a theatrical trunk jammed with fanciful costumes. She clung to it in the event her voice returned. Sometimes, in a festive mood, she would fling open the lid and dress up to amuse her young sons with full-throated theatrics.

She was a flamboyant actress and a dramatic reader. Hoping for cosmic help to restore her voice, she had turned to religion, attaching herself to the Church of England. Chaplin recalled one early evening when he was recovering from a fever and she picked up the Bible.

"She gave the most luminous and appealing interpretation of Christ that I have ever heard or seen. . . . She read into the dusk, stopping only to light the lamp, then told of the faith that Jesus inspired in the sick, that they had only to touch the hem of His garment to be healed. . . ."

She acted out "His arrest and His calm dignity before Pontius Pilate, who, washing his hands, said (this she acted out histrioni- cally): 'I find no fault with this man.'

"She told how they stripped and scourged Him and, placing a crown of thorns on His head, mocked and spat at Him, saying: 'Hail, King of the Jews!'

"As she continued, tears welled up in her eyes. . . . And in His last dying agony crying out: 'My God, why hast Thou forsaken me?' And we both wept.

"Mother had so carried me away that I wanted to die that very night and meet Jesus."

It was all his mother could do to persuade her weeping child to remain awhile longer among the living. She couldn't have contrived a stronger example of the conjuring power of a story stoked with emotion and brilliantly acted. These became the muscles of Chaplin's films, as yet offstage and unimagined.

As Hannah's prayers became more intense, religion soon replaced her old footlight world and the gaiety of theater friends. She cut up a velvet stage jacket with pleated, colored sleeves to make a coat for Sydney, already in school; an oddity he refused to wear except in tears.

She cut down a pair of red tights into baggy stockings for Charlie. He had grown old enough to sense the doom descending like a first-act curtain on their lives. He remembered seeing her as silent as a still life as she sat for three days staring out the window.

She bestirred herself to petition for child support for her two boys, but the senior Charles showed no interest and dodged the law.

"Like sand in an hourglass our finances ran out," remarked the actor who would become the envy of the world. "We existed in a cheerless twilight."

And the first signs of Hannah's impending madness revealed itself. In midsummer, she was discovered wrapping single lumps of coal to make birthday gifts for the neighbors.

She was admitted to the Lambeth infirmary. Charlie was yanked out of school and, together with Sydney, moved to the nearby workhouse.

The gloomy brick workhouse of Charlie's childhood.

CHAPTER THREE
LIFE IN THE BOOBY HATCH

THERE, OVERLOOKING NOTHING, STOOD THE smoke-darkened brick buildings for the poor. It was 1896. The workhouse years, for Chaplin, were adventures in humiliation and loneliness.

He and Sydney were ushered through the iron gate to the Lambeth fortress of charity. They qualified "owing to the absence of their father and the destitution and illness of their mother," said the ledger entry.

Hannah was immediately separated from her sons and disappeared into the women's ward. A couple of weeks later, the boys were transported by a horse-drawn bakery van to the Hanwell Schools for Orphans and Destitute Children. Sydney was plucked off to join the big boys, Charlie to go with the infants. For the first time in his life, Charlie was entirely alone. He was a little over six.

Charlie could not be unaware that in being a child of the work-house he was wearing a raw brand on his forehead—P for Poor. Neighbors smirked at the place, nicknaming it the Booby Hatch.

To his acute embarrassment, his head was shaved in an assault against ringworm. His lifeline was an occasional glimpse of eleven-year-old Sydney, who worked in the kitchen. Now and then he was able to slip Charlie a roll with a Himalayan lump of butter in it.

The reigning nightmare was the 200-pound ex-navy drill master, a Captain Hindom, whose high rank was self-bestowed. Every week the schoolboys were gathered to watch in horror as he flogged a derelict child with swift lashes of a cane or birch.

Charlie himself fell victim to the captain's righteous beatings. He had chosen not to betray a couple of boys who had set some bits of paper on fire in the boys' room.

When Sydney saw his little brother's bottom exposed across the drill master's fat knees and lashed by the cane, he burst into tears.

Despite the drill master's command of terror, Charlie adjusted to school. It fascinated him to learn to write his own name. It was better wizardry than the coin trick! He learned that at Christmas he could look forward to the treasure of a fresh orange. He imagined carefully peeling it, and dividing the segments so as not to lose a single drop of juice. He planned to hoard the treat to make it last for several days. Alas, it was discovered that he had failed to make up his bed that morning, and so no orange or stick of candy would be his that Christmas. The memory and the pain endured for a lifetime.

In the years ahead, he would boomerang in and out of the work-houses. He summed up the underlying soul and temper of his life in a word: "sadness."

The only prank he could recall was rebellion with a smile. Sydney conceived an escape plan that Hannah conspired in and that would take a bit of acting. Putting on airs of a change in fortune, she checked herself and the boys out of the workhouse and its schools. Charlie recalled their day together in the park, playing catch with newspaper balled up and tied with a string. They blew their fortune wrapped in a handkerchief, a few copper coins, on a half pound of cherries and shared cups of tea.

Then Hannah blithely checked everyone back into the institution, where all the original admittance paperwork had to be repeated. The staff was not amused. But, if only for a tender, indelible day, the small family had been reunited.

Charlie at school, age seven and a half. He is circled in the photo, third row from the bottom, sixth from the left.

It was the loss of Sydney's close company that most profoundly affected Charlie. Poverty had bound them together as tightly as mismatched Siamese twins. Boys from the charity schools were recruited for training aboard a decommissioned navy ship. Sydney was growing tall and muscular, and was chosen. One day he vanished.

Charlie was left to survive entirely alone. Hannah let more than a painful year go by without visiting him. His feelings of abandonment forged into shyness and quietness. But he also grew chain mail on his skinny boy's armor. It would see him through the duels and ambushes lying dead ahead.

During that time, a reward was offered for information leading to the arrest of the senior Chaplin for failing to support his sons. The guardians of the law had only to venture across the river to the disreputable London theater district to find the deadbeat thespian for themselves.

But it was January of the following year, 1898, before the reluctant parent was arrested. He managed to raise the fine. Two days later Sydney was discharged from his training ship, where he had learned to blow the bugle. He hung around, fruitlessly awaiting sea duty.

In the fall, Hannah went mad and was carried off to the asylum. Charlie reacted with "baffling despair." He wrote, "Why had she

CHAPTER FOUR

LIFE WITH FATHER

ONE WONDERS IF THE BREAD VAN HAD TIME FOR the bakery, for it seemed forever on the road with the Chaplin brothers. Now it delivered them like shabbily wrapped packages to their father in a two-room upstairs apartment on respectable Kennington Road.

True to form, the senior Chaplin managed to be absent for the occasion. But the woman in his life, Louise, signed receipts for the two boys, and survival in the domestic trenches began.

Wrote Chaplin: "Everything looked as sad as Louise; the wallpaper looked sad, the horsehair furniture looked sad, and the stuffed pike in a glass case that had swallowed another pike as large as itself—the head sticking out of its mouth—looked gruesomely sad."

And Louise drank.

She was certainly unhappy to have two boys thrust into her home. She had put a bed for them in the back room, but it was too small for two. When Sydney complained and offered to sleep on a sofa in the living room, she laid down the law. "You'll sleep where you're told to," she sizzled.

When the older Chaplin returned home to greet his sons, he learned of the tempest and decreed that Sydney should move to the sofa. Louise's resentment rose to the boiling point and stuck there.

She shuffled Charlie off to school, to be rid of him. He recalled returning home hungry but finding no food in the place. The apartment was deserted. He waited, growing ever more famished.

Like a caged animal, Charlie was untrained in hunting his own food. He ventured to the nearby markets and gazed at joints of beef and potatoes in Turkish baths of steaming gravy. His hunger became painful.

He sat on the curb, a forlorn nine-year-old. He was accustomed to Sydney's staying out late, but where was everyone else? Had they deserted him?

It was long past dark when he saw Louise coming along. She appeared to have lost her alignment with gravity. She was walking lopsided. She was drunk.

"I had never seen a lopsided drunk before," he wrote. Nothing would escape notice that he could build on later. He learned and practiced. For years, in the theater, he excelled at playing a falling-down inebriate.

Choosing to avoid Louise, he paused before following her into the house. As if in wait, she staggered out to the head of the stairs.

"Where the hell do you think you're going?" she said. "This is not your home."

I stood motionless.

"You're not sleeping here tonight. I've had enough of all of you. Get out! You and your brother!"

His hunger vanished. He turned and fled onto the street. His father was likely attending one of his favorite pubs. Half a mile away, Charlie found him bursting out of the Queen's Head.

"'She won't let me in,' I whimpered." His father, too, he saw, couldn't walk a straight line without help.

But his aim was good when they reached home. He threw a clothes brush, striking Louise on the head and knocking her out.

Charlie was stunned to see the arrival of fury in his father's ice blue eyes and the violence in his behavior. Any flowering respect vanished.

It would not be the first night Louise shut Charlie and Sydney out of the house. Later, the police found them trying to sleep near a small street fire to keep warm. The Society for the Prevention of Cruelty to Children paid an ominous call on her.

She was rescued when Hannah knocked at the door, freed from the asylum. She had come to collect her two boys. Charlie fell into her arms and ran to gather his things. Unlike the fish being eaten alive by another in the front room, he was escaping with his young life.

He was to write that the workhouse years were a stick of candy compared to the two months of life with Father on Kennington Road. Life with Mother would resume, this time in the basement room behind the smelly pickle factory and next to the smellier slaughterhouse.

Charles Chaplin
Father of Charlie

H.T. REED   LONDON

Charlie Chaplin, Sr.—the man Charlie grew up believing to be his father. Later, the comedian had his doubts.

Charlie lived with his mother and brother in a room at the end of this street, behind a pickle factory and next to a slaughterhouse.

Chapter Five
POSTER BOY

CHARLIE COULD REMEMBER THE FIRST TIME laughter burst past his one or two missing teeth. Every day, sheep would be driven past the house to the slaughter building. When one of the animals escaped, the neighborhood kids joined in a slapstick capture, laughing and chasing the frightened beast. Charlie was among them, as noisy as the rest.

Only after the excitement died down did he stop to realize the tragedy lying in wait behind the slaughterhouse doors. The rebellious sheep would be butchered. He burst into tears and ran to his mother. "They're going to kill it!"

He would never forget how quickly laughter and tears changed places. He saw that they shot like geysers from a common source. As if privy to a great secret, he built his greatest comedies on it. In his first big feature-length hit, *The Kid*, a child is hunted down to be carried off to the orphanage. What's so funny about that? Trust him.

Hannah took up the needle again, to do piecework for sweat-shop wages. Sydney got a job at the post office. Charlie unhappily returned to school. He was an inattentive scholar; the only value he could see in arithmetic was to protect him "against being short-changed." As for history, he was more excited by fancy than facts. He chose the improvisations of playing hooky.

He enjoyed the street entertainments. He earned throw money by clog dancing, a popular form of dancing in wooden clogs with the arms held rigidly at the sides and the feet and legs doing all the work. He washed in a horse trough outside a stable. Decades later, famous at last, he returned to the scenes of his childhood and saw the trough, still standing.

As bewitching as a shooting star, a theater poster redirected his young life. The proprietor of a vaudeville troop of clog-dancing boys called the Eight Lancaster Lads faced a dilemma. His supply of expensive posters said eight. Unfortunately, Mr. Jackson had only seven lads.

It would be cheaper to hire a new lad than to go back to the printer for new posters. Charlie got the job, and his mother would be paid most of his earnings each week. He would receive free room and board and a suit of clothes to perform in.

What he thought of having to wear a lace collar, velvet pants, and red shoes, he left unsaid. But the outfit had the virtue of being the newest wardrobe he'd ever worn.

Charlie was rehearsed in the routines of the act and went before the footlights as a professional entertainer a few weeks later. To save money on makeup, Mr. Jackson lined up the lads and pinched their cheeks to make their smiles rosy.

The reviews were strong. "Eight perfectly drilled lads, who treat the audience to some of the finest clog dancing it is possible to imagine," wrote a London critic.

The precision of the act came at a cost of long, tiring hours of rehearsal. A few years later, Chaplin told a reporter in Winnipeg, Canada, "Sometimes we would almost fall asleep on the stage." He was soon picking up juggling and acrobatic tricks and discovering that he was hardly more educated than a turnip. He was on a theater bill with an actor bringing to the stage various characters from the famous novels by Charles Dickens. Audiences were thrilled and applauded the artist to exhaustion. Charlie didn't understand what the fuss was about.

He bought a copy of Dickens's *Oliver Twist*, though he was barely literate enough to turn the pages, and stowed away on a voyage of self-education. Later and offstage, he could almost always be found struggling through a book. His ambitions had taken a profound shift. Performing was necessary for fried bread and haddock. He would spend a lifetime pursuing a closeted aspiration to become well educated. An intellectual.

In the back of his mind lay a nightmare in ambush: Might his mother again go mad? And on her part, Hannah's maternal concern was aroused: Charlie was looking pale and worn-out. Clog dancing was bad for the lungs, she foolishly insisted. Her complaints became such a persistent noise for Mr. Jackson that in 1901 he fired Charlie.

After two years and four months, the curtain fell on Chaplin's stage career. Clog dancing proved to be no more than passing employment. His dream of becoming a boy comedian failed to reach the stage. Forgetting this early ambition, he would confess to shifting delusions some years later. "The last thing I dreamed of was becoming a comedian. My idea was to be a Member of Parliament or a great musician . . . The only thing I really dreamed about was being rich. We were so poor that wealth seemed to me to be the summit."

With Sydney hired on as a bugler aboard a passenger ship to

South Africa, and the clog money up in smoke, Hannah moved her family again, this time to a room next to a graveyard. The view lacked a certain cheer, and they carried their furnishings to a room above a barbershop. There Charlie got a job lathering the faces of clients in preparation for the skilled razor.

Chaplin's head began to fill with get-rich-quick schemes. He'd start a business. All he lacked was a grubstake.

He talked his mother into allowing him to quit school at age eleven to give him a head start on the ladder to success. He got work as an errand boy, a receptionist, a janitor in a doctor's office, and a glass blower, where he fainted from the heat and lasted one day. He landed a position as page boy in a home that could afford harmless pretensions. So impressed was he with the elegance that he had fantasies of growing up to become a butler.

After several weeks, with success ever distant and elusive, Hannah put him back in school. How would he ever get anywhere with that voice of his? It was bad enough to be a Cockney without speaking like one. School was failing to filter out his accent. She was forever correcting his tonal and grammatical abuses. He was, after all, the son of actors.

Before long, in an accident of time and place, Charlie pleased his father by performing some bits in a nearby tavern. He was startled to feel the senior Charles give him a hug and a kiss, the first and only embrace in his memory.

But it was too late to repair the years of damage, for Charlie was never to see him again. Although clearly ill, the senior Chaplin refused help. Friends had to get him first topped off with gin in order to get him to the hospital. There, in 1901, he died. A wealthy younger brother paid for a showy funeral. At long last, the failing actor was cast as a leading man in a show. There was standing room only.

Hannah, still the legal wife of the deceased, inherited his fortune—a bloodstained suit, an old dressing gown, and a pair of plaid house slippers. The heirs found an orange curiously stuffed in the toes.

When the mourners extracted the fruit, out tumbled a gold coin. It was providence! It was capital! Charlie immediately ran off to go into business.

At the flower market he "purchased two bundles of narcissus, and after school busied myself making them into penny bundles."

With black crepe on his arm and the flowers of death in hand, he would pop in and out of saloons. "The women always responded:

'Who is it, son?' And I would lower my voice to a whisper: 'My father.'"

He was able to return home and shower a rattle of coins before his mother. When she discovered the money had come from bar-rooms, she put an end to the enterprise. Money from those sinful sources rubbed her religious scruples the wrong way. But she kept the jackpot.

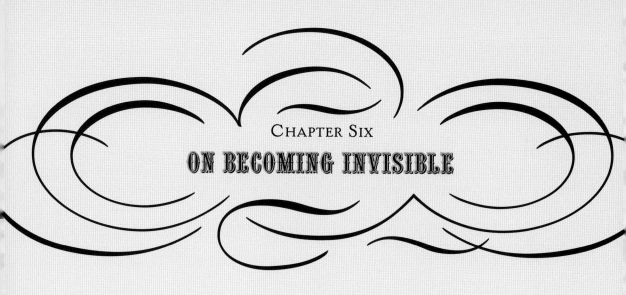

CHAPTER SIX
ON BECOMING INVISIBLE

ONCE AGAIN, HANNAH WENT MAD.

With Sydney at sea again, Charlie alone remained to look after her. She leaned on him as, shaky from malnutrition, she had to tramp the mile to the nearest medical help. The next day she would be sent to the asylum, twenty miles away.

When Charlie returned home, he could find no food in the cupboard except a package of tea. Her purse on the mantel disclosed several pawn tickets and three small coins.

The landlady said he could stay in the room until she rented it. His great fear now was to be sent back to the workhouse.

He would need to make himself invisible. "I would steal out in the early morning and stay out all day," he recalled.

If only Sydney would return! Charlie became a vagabond of

the city, hardly bothering to wash in the horse trough outside the stable. His curly hair grew into a nest of black snakes. And Sydney failed to show up. He was weeks overdue.

Charlie discovered men as rough as tree bark on the city outskirts—woodchoppers. He got a job helping to gather the wood into small bundles. The laborers proved to be a quiet but affable lot, and the new helper was well fed, even allowed to join them to see a music hall show. On the bill was Fred Karno's vaudeville act. A few years dead ahead, Charlie would be playing a comedy drunk in Karno's newest hit show. The skit would carry the performing troop to New York and Charlie to Hollywood. He hadn't yet a clue of what the tea leaves had in store for him.

Charlie dodged in and out of the unrented room, for Sydney might turn up any day. One late night, the landlady stopped him on his way up the stairs. A telegram had come. Sydney would arrive at the Waterloo train station at ten o'clock the next day.

The two brothers saw each other and collided like freight trains. When Sydney saw Charlie's dirty clothes, ragged hair, and shoe top about to flap open like the jaws of a crocodile, he knew their mother wouldn't have allowed him out. Not in public, looking like this. "What's happened?" he asked.

Charlie held nothing back. "Mother went insane." He told his brother she'd been moved to the asylum miles away.

Sydney absorbed the news silently. He hired a horse-drawn cab and loaded his belongings, including a stalk of green bananas from the tropics. He was abandoning the sea, he said, and had saved a bankroll large enough to support the two of them for the next five months. Meanwhile, he intended to get work. He had decided to become an actor.

When they returned to the streets to give Charlie a wash and to get his hair cut, Sydney bought him a new suit of clothes. The next day they made the long trip to visit their mother.

As they left, she said, "If only you had given me a cup of tea that afternoon I would have been all right."

For the rest of his life, Charlie tried to understand the disordered mystery behind her complaint.

CHAPTER SEVEN

ENTER, SHERLOCK HOLMES

IF CHARLIE HAD HEARD OF FAUST, WHO MADE A pact with the devil to exchange his soul for recaptured youth and other yearnings, the Cockney would have been glad to make the trade. All he yearned for was a change in luck and maybe a kidney pie. The change arrived, anyway, and haggle free.

If Sydney would be an actor, why not Charlie? In his new clothes and with his hair slicked down, the younger Chaplin, too, ventured into the theatrical agencies seeking a boy's part in any play being cast.

Lo and behold! A month of persistence and there came a postcard from H. Blakemore's, a prestigious agency across the river. Charlie was commanded to return to the office.

He was offered the role of a page boy, a servant in a wealthy household, in a Sherlock Holmes stage mystery based on Sir Arthur Conan

Doyle's fabled detective. He was handed a script on the spot. Charlie's heart sank. If the people asked him to read his significant role—page after page of it—they'd discover his secret. He could barely read.

Fortunately, the play wouldn't be going into rehearsal for a week and Charlie was advised to study his part at home. He took a breath at last. Sydney would help him with the script. The acting he was sure he could handle by luck and instinct.

On the bus home, he would later write, "I realized I had crossed an important threshold. No longer was I a nondescript of the slums; now I was a personage of the theater. I wanted to weep." With Sydney reading to him, Charlie learned the thirty-five "sides"— pages of his part—by heart in three days.

He would receive a bountiful two pounds, ten shillings a week. Given more than a century of inflation, the sum flowers into a hundred dollars or so. He and Sydney could live like princes, but they remained frugal. What if the play was a flop?

Before Charlie left to tour with the play, he and Sydney visited Hannah, only to find her confined to a padded cell. Charlie hesitated to see her brought so woefully low, but the nurse was reassuring. Mrs. Chaplin had brightened and was rational.

Charlie sat together with his mother on a heavily padded cot. When he rose to leave, she reinforced his own fears with a whisper.

"Don't lose your way, because they might keep you here."

The doctors kept her there for another seven months.

CHAPTER EIGHT

DON'T MUG TOO MUCH

THE SHERLOCK HOLMES SHOW WAS A 1903 SMASH hit. After the first year's run of the show, Charlie was signed for a second. He was a dazzler on stage, handsome and saucy. The producer who first cast an eye on him had detected the glow of talent stored like tinder wood beneath the charming but shy Cockney kid. All the talent had needed was the bellows of a play to ignite it into flames with puffs of oxygen.

And Charlie was now discovering an unknown world of the actor's craft—timing, the pause, performing on cue. The star of the show could hardly believe that Charlie had never before acted. But "I mugged too much when I talked," Chaplin later wrote.

By keeping his eyes open, he picked up the stage art of slapstick comedy—trips and pratfalls, collisions and tumbles. He proved to be a natural at physical humor. A born acrobat.

Charlie learned his new arts as if he had a streetcar to catch. He was in a hurry to make the world notice him.

He was now fifteen and still fit his page boy costume. He was growing as slowly as an oak, and would soon top out at barely five feet, four inches. With his narrow build and small hands and feet, he gave the impression of being even smaller. After an interview, the writer Alistair Cooke wrote, "He certainly is a tiny man."

Sydney hadn't been lucky enough to land an acting job. Charlie got him a small role in the second year of the Holmes drama. When the play closed, Charlie was shocked to discover that he was not as famous as he had supposed. Unable to find a better job, he signed for a third season with Sherlock Holmes, but with a third-rate company and at vastly reduced wages. "It was a depressing comedown," he recalled.

Soon he was discovering for himself the life of an actor. He was out of work for ten months.

During those bleak times, the budding impresario in him envisioned gold pieces growing on the theatrical tree. All he had to do was make up with whiskers and pretend to be an old Jew to pluck the treasure. He'd give it a try. "At that time Jewish comedians were all the rage in London," he wrote.

After all, he had a connection to the Jewish people, didn't he? Wasn't Sydney half Jewish? That gambler their mother had run off with to South Africa, she said he was Jewish.

Charlie worked up some funny songs and bought an American joke book. He combed through it for Jewish humor.

He practiced this new act, making up as a stereotypical bent and greedy Jew, a joke-telling Fagin, the leader of the gang of boy pickpockets in Dickens's *Oliver Twist*.

Trying out the act, he offered his talents free of charge to a theater in a heavily Jewish quarter of London. "Within a year I might rise to be one of vaudeville's biggest headliners," he convinced himself.

It would have been easier to become the King of England. His jokes shocked and enraged the audience. They began throwing orange peels and any other garbage at hand. The theater vibrated with the stamping of feet that might rise at any moment and kick him off the British Isles.

In Charlie's innocence, he used jokes he had found in the American joke book that were anti-Semitic. They were exceeded in their insult only by his insensitive accent and heavy-handed makeup. He fled the theater, barely pausing to collect his music.

This would not be Charlie's last tempest in matters Jewish. Given his complexion, darker than anyone else's in the family, his curly hair and short stature, he was sometimes taken to be part Jewish. His denials were models of kindness and generosity. "I don't have that honor," was his frequent reply.

Nevertheless, the suspicion followed him around with the persistence of a horsefly.

CHAPTER NINE
A RED NOSE

EANWHILE, SYDNEY FOUND A JOB AS A knockabout performer in vaudeville and got Charlie through the stage door to opportunity. He arranged a meeting with Fred Karno, whose comedy act Charlie had seen when he was learning the humble art of wood chopping.

Karno, a former acrobat grown round as a soccer ball, gave Charlie a two-week tryout. If the kid proved out, he would get a year's contract.

A chastised Charlie fled jokes for visual humor. "I had already discovered the secret of being funny . . . an idea going in one direction hits an opposite idea," he revealed. To this end, he invented a lifetime of slapstick variations on the classic laugh getter, slipping on a banana peel.

In other words, he looked for an idea to woefully collide with the basic situation. None of his later films would be without the opposing "nightmare," as Chaplin often called the technique. Escaping through a window, the tramp discovers a policeman on duty below. While he is balancing himself on a high wire in a circus, escaped monkeys climb all over him. Conflict! Conflict!

He seemed to be a stylist from the beginning. Almost every movement he made, from tipping his hat to shuffling cards to counting a stack of bills at the speed of a propeller, was Chaplinesque.

Already a master of surprise, he was to play a villain in a sketch about bribing a football team. His inventive mind provided him with an entrance that set off a first laugh within seconds.

The curtains parted on a gym set. Enter an elegantly dressed Charlie in top hat, frock coat, and spats—his back to the audience. Then he pivoted around, revealing an alcoholic red nose.

Crossing the stage, he tripped over a dumbbell. Recovering his dignity, he managed to catch his cane on the punching bag. On rebound, it punches him. He swings at it with his cane, succeeding only in striking his own face. A fifth laugh in a minute or so.

When portly Karno saw the new kid, so shy offstage and so funny on, he rushed to get Charlie's signature on a contract.

By this time Charlie and Sydney, like their mother, had moved and moved again. But now it was a different story, for they were changing to ever grander neighborhoods. They put in Turkish carpets and hired a maid. Said Chaplin, "We wanted to slough our skins, shedding every vestige of the past." This became a theme of his long life.

What about Hannah? After a few months of recovery, she had to be readmitted to the asylum, suffering from delusions, agitation, and disorientation. This time she was confined for seven and a half years.

Charlie was not the first great movie comedian lurking among Karno's troupe of comedians. Stan Laurel, soon to become famous in the team of Laurel and Hardy, recalled nineteen-year-old Chaplin. "He appeared stand-offish. He wasn't, he wasn't at all . . . he is a very, very shy man." And of Karno's influence on them both: "He didn't teach Charlie and me everything we knew about comedy. He just taught us most of it."

The slapstick maestro drilled them for six months to achieve perfect timing and ease and precision. And each comedian, recalled Chaplin, had to master a repertoire of parts so that the players could stand in for one another when necessary.

Charlie was not yet twenty when he found himself in fabled Paris. Karno had booked a skit into the gilt-and-plush Folies Bergère.

Almost as good as getting his name in lights, Chaplin gets two pictures of himself on this advertising piece, third down and bottom center. Smiling on the bottom right is Stan Laurel, soon to become a movie star himself.

Charlie was thrilled. For the first time he found himself in a foreign land and was soon on the boulevards, sitting at the sidewalk tables as confidently as any Frenchman. On the other hand, he met Claude Debussy and didn't have a clue who the great composer was.

He would learn. Later, at a book stall in New York, he would buy used textbooks—to teach himself grammar and rhetoric—and most ambitiously, a Latin-English dictionary. One can only guess what he intended to do with it. Hit Karno over the head with Ovid in the original language?

That Charlie was in Manhattan at all was due to Karno's failure to fatten his salary. In Europe, their contract had been expiring, and the skinny kid had demanded a raise. In what appears to have been a put-up job, Karno phoned a theater manager and let the comedian listen in.

Said Karno, "I understand you did poor business last week."

"Lousy!" came a voice.

Karno grinned. "What about Chaplin, the principal comedian? Wasn't he any good?"

"He stinks!" said the voice.

Charlie refused to have his talent insulted. He snatched the phone and, before Karno could grab it back, shouted, "Maybe he stinks, but not half as much as your stinkpot theatre."

Karno hung up the phone before the hotheaded kid could expand on the theme. Charlie then threatened to rip up the contract, but Karno was too shrewd to let one of his prize fish off the line. He agreed to raise the salary from five to six English pounds a week. With riches like that, Charlie could afford a new pair of high-button shoes with spats and a brown derby hat.

Karno chose to send him across the Atlantic to New York City, where the promoter's vaudeville comedies were popular. Charlie would have to earn his new six pounds a week.

When he first laid eyes on New York in the chilly fall days of 1910, Chaplin felt an emotion generally assigned to the genders: He experienced love at first sight. He loved the classless society, the tall buildings, and opportunity beckoning everywhere. And like a heaven of its own, lightbulbs blazed away like a vast, municipal Milky Way. "This is it!" he told himself. "This is where I belong!"

With sudden conviction, he decided to move again—this time to America.

The English troupe was a headline attraction in New York. After a week of rehearsal, it became apparent to Charlie that his love for the big city might be unrequited if he couldn't rise above his material.

The troupe of Karno comedians sails to America. Chaplin makes it clear that he is the star of the show by featuring himself through the life preserver. Stan Laurel is the second actor to Chaplin's right.

In a camping scene, Charlie as Archie enters holding a teacup.

ARCHIE: "Good morning, Hudson. Do you mind giving me a little water?"

HUDSON: "Certainly. What do you want it for?"

ARCHIE: "I want to take a bath."

This opening was a huge laugh in England. It hardly unleashed a snicker from the audience of New Yorkers, few of whom had ever been camping.

HUDSON: "How did you sleep last night, Archie?"

ARCHIE: "Oh, terribly. I dreamt I was being chased by a caterpillar."

A graveyard silence settled over the audience. Night after night the actors chattered on, to the annoyance of the audience.

With his pantomime comedy, he alone of the entire company won the approval of the show-business paper *Variety*, which singled him out as the only funny Englishman in the bunch.

By a quirk of fate, a booking agent was in the theater along with an audience made up of a contingent of English butlers and valets. The exiles howled at the jokes. The clueless agent booked the troupe for a twenty-week cross-country tour; its escape back to England would be delayed.

Charlie found himself gazing at the country on a train heading west. He was barely aware that they made movies out in California. He was more interested in the perpetual sunshine.

CHAPTER TEN

THE TIPSY GENTLEMAN

LIKE MANY SHY TEENAGERS, CHARLIE WAS A loner. That he had few friends was confirmed by his obsessions. At age sixteen he bought a violin and later a cello and began practicing from four to six hours a day. The screech of scales and pizzicati in his private life not only kept friends at bay but isolated him from bill collectors.

Over the horizon, he saw himself graduating from slapstick comedian to concert artist. Devotedly taking his instruments on tour, he would arrange for lessons from string players or conductors in the theater pit orchestras.

It was a little late to become a child prodigy, but he'd hurry. He knew from discipline with the Karno show the payoff of patient and constant rehearsal: exquisite skill. Only practice would

In his early vaudeville days, he traveled light, with three pieces of luggage—his beloved cello, a violin, and a small case with little in it but an extra pair of socks and a spare shirt. As he was left-handed, his musical instruments were strung backward.

produce the bewitchment of the fingers he needed for the concert stage. It was of little consequence that, being left-handed, he was obliged to string his instruments in reverse order—that is to say, upside down—while playing the music right side up.

On the tour west, Stan Laurel recalled being assigned Chaplin and his violin as roommates. He was, in fact, Charlie's understudy. How the gentle comedian arranged to go deaf whenever Charlie opened his instrument case, he doesn't say, unless it was to take four- to six-hour walks.

Reaching the orange trees of California, Charlie was earning $75 a week. Living frugally, he banked every spare penny. The amateur businessman in him saw a fortune to be made in raising hogs, and he offered to put up $2,000 in partnership with a knowledgeable Westerner. But his passion for books sank the deal. In a tome on pig raising, he read with horror the details of farm surgeries he would be expected to perform on the male piglets, and he ran for the exit.

His other reading fed a deeper need. He would not allow himself to stumble through life as an ignorant Cockney. He discovered Ralph Waldo Emerson and was engaged by the freethinking views of Robert Ingersoll. A freethinker, that's what he aspired to be. He pursued German philosopher Arthur Schopenhauer in three barely penetrable volumes. He consumed the Americans Edgar Allan Poe, Nathaniel Hawthorne, Washington Irving, and Mark Twain.

Meanwhile, the manager of the road company substituted the vaudeville skit for one with more appeal to American audiences. Charlie was given a new role that would jump-start a new career.

He impersonated a well-dressed but tipsy gentleman in a number called "A Night in an English Music Hall." The absurd, wobbly behavior of comic drunks was a standard laugh getter. Charlie would make his rendering memorable.

A slight twenty-one-year-old who looked older in makeup, Charlie bewildered the other acts when he wasn't carted off to the hospital after every performance. How could he make so many trips and falls without breaking a leg, an arm, or his spirit?

For those who could afford them, theaters were built with private boxes, like small parlors above stage level, along the walls. In his drunk act, Charlie enters to seat himself in a theater box, pausing first, with great dignity, to peel off a white glove. Moments later, too hazy to remember, he again attempts to remove the glove. He tries to light his cigar from an electric light. When a stooge in the next box strikes a match for him, Charlie reaches for it with his cigar and falls out of the box.

Charlie's gift for constant invention reveals itself. He climbs back into the box, only to balance out and hang on again, feet dangling. The audience gasps. Physical humor is triumphant. At the climax, the diminutive drunk finds himself onstage wrestling a huge and terrible villain.

Charlie was an enormous hit, even though some audiences took the inebriated man in the box to be an obnoxious paying customer. American vaudeville demanded three shows a day, giving Charlie an opportunity to polish his comic drunk to a high glow.

The first advertisements for the show gave sole credit for the skit to modest Fred Karno in huge letters. By the time the western tour wrapped up and returned to New York, the advertisement had changed, and Chaplin now captured top billing.

Unbeknownst to Charlie, he had caught the eye of a star maker. Mack Sennett, regarded as the king of film comedy, had been in the audience in New York. Later, Sennett remembered:

"I was impressed, more than impressed. Stunned might be a good word . . . a little fellow who could move like a ballet dancer. The next week I couldn't remember his name but . . . I never forgot that wonderful easy grace of movement. I had seen nothing like it. I've seen nothing like it since . . . "

A year or so would pass before the English stage drunk crossed his mind.

Meanwhile, still tied by contract to Karno, Charlie returned to London, where he discovered that Sydney had married and that their bachelor lodgings with the Turkish carpets and the maid were a thing of the past. Charlie moved once again.

Visiting Hannah, he was confronted and pained once more by a mother restrained in a padded cell. She had continued to be violent and had undergone shock treatments. Now that they could afford it, he arranged with Sydney to have her moved to a private hospital.

Karno kept Charlie busy in England, delaying the comedian's return to New York until 1912.

Playing in Philadelphia the following year, Charlie was handed a mysterious telegram by the company manager.

"Is there a man named Chaffin in your company or something like that stop if so will he communicate with . . . "

It was a representative of Mack Sennett, he of the faulty memory, seeking to find the tipsy gentleman in the theater box.

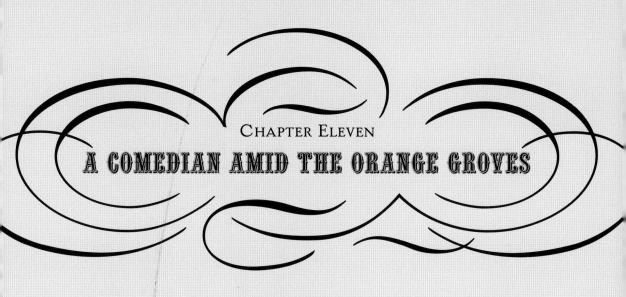

CHAPTER ELEVEN

A COMEDIAN AMID THE ORANGE GROVES

MACK SENNETT WAS A HUSKY CANADIAN AND former burlesque comedian whose taste in humor was characterized by the elegance of his movie invention—the custard pie in the face.

He had lifted himself to eminence by the bootstraps of his company of gifted slapstick comedians. He had launched the wildly popular Keystone Cops, who tripped through miles of film footage chasing villains. He would make film stars of such royalty of the silents as Gloria Swanson, Roscoe "Fatty" Arbuckle, and Marie Dressler. Now he was on the trail of Charlie Chaplin, whom he had seen onstage in the character of an older man.

Charlie responded to the telegram. The Keystone managers were offering him $150 a week—twice what Karno was paying him. He had merely to come back to California, pick an orange, and go into pictures. It was a greater sum than had ever before been dangled in front of his eyes. That didn't stop him from boldly and successfully negotiating a raise. After a three-month trial period, he could expect to see his paychecks bumped up to $175.

He was still under contract to Karno and had to play out the clock. Finally, in the fall of 1913, he cut his London lifeline and hopped a train to Los Angeles, a Spanish town grown big, with sagebrush and tumbleweed still sticking out of its ears.

He knew, at twenty-four, that he had caught the gold ring. Charlie's inner Paganini ran through his last capriccio and retired his violin and cello.

Chapter Twelve
THE GALLOPING TINTYPES

THE STORY OF CHAPLIN'S STRAIGHT-CUT LITTLE mustache began when he arrived in Los Angeles. His burly new boss regarded him in alarm. Mack Sennett thought he had hired a savvy stage veteran. Before him stood a shy youth who might not have enough movie sense to steal a scene. "I thought you were a much older man."

"I can make up as old as you like," Charlie answered defensively. He'd been through this when first meeting Karno. Again? But this time the remark would have a kickback effect.

The Keystone studio, Chaplin discovered, stood in the farm fields of the San Fernando Valley, some five miles from downtown Los Angeles. He hopped a streetcar to a rent-cheap enclave named Edendale that was regarded as the film capital. Hollywood was

The Keystone Studio at the time Charlie took up picture-making there. Movie audiences were as movie-struck with cars as comedy props in 1914 as they are today with automobile crashes. Chaplin managed to get two reels of laughter out of the internal combustion machine in his 1919 film *A Day's Pleasure*.

Only ghosts in comic makeup remain in what had been the fabled Keystone Studio, now a storage facility.

then no more than a pretentious real estate sign high on the other side of the hills.

Along Edendale's main drag hunched studio after studio lined up like livestock at the trough, there to feed on the eternal sunshine for their cameras. Tom Mix westerns, like other hoof-and-mouth dramas, were made among the rattlesnakes in the surrounding sagebrush.

The brain trust of the Keystone comedy factory lived amid the glamour of a down-at-the-heels four-room bungalow. A ramshackle barn served for dressing rooms. A green fence ran around the property, as much to keep the film clowns in as visitors out.

This small movie world was as mysterious to Charlie as the dark side of the moon. He was seized with a panic of shyness and fled on a streetcar back to his hotel. His courage returned the next day.

The stage, he saw, was strangely wide open to the elements. The hot sun came beating through white linen yardage drawn like mosquito netting around the long shooting platform, some two blocks long. There stood "a wilderness of 'sets'—drawing rooms, prison interiors, laundries, balconies, staircases, caves, fire escapes, kitchens, cellars." The diffused light served the cameras at a time when Edison's incandescent bulbs had not yet displaced the sun in movie lighting.

Since the camera was deaf, sound was not a factor. Three or four different films might be shooting, side by side, on the same stage. Noise and chaos were Keystone's proof that the studio was putting its best footage forward.

When it came time for Charlie to go before the cameras, Sennett introduced the man who would direct his first film, a former streetcar conductor named Henry Lehrman. He had bluffed his way into movie making. His guiding theory held forth that "comedy is an excuse for a chase." With Chaplin's lifetime passion for character and nuance, Lehrman's grasp of movies as galloping tintypes could hardly cohabit the same set. There was bound to be friction.

Sennett told Charlie to go inside a nearby building, put together a costume, and be ready to shoot.

Shoot? Where was the script?

Keystone provided no scripts. Sennett would verbally fling forth a bare-bones storyline cobbled together by his writers, who rarely touched the typewriter. The director was expected to fill one or two reels of film—a total of ten or twelve minutes of playing time per reel—improvising from first take to last.

Silent dialogue flashed on the screen to help the story along was regarded as a pox unless a laugh could be squeezed out of the text.

Said D. W. Griffith, the Moses of early filmmakers, handing down one of his commandments, "People don't come to the movies to read. They come to look at pictures."

All Charlie knew was that he was to play a rascally newspaper reporter out to scoop a rival. He slipped into a villainous-looking frock coat and a foppish top hat to match.

Lehrman ran out of ideas, Chaplin recalled. Always quick to improvise, the newcomer was happy to offer a few of his own. All had a comic flare.

Charlie had not counted on the director's inflammable vanity. "This was where I created antagonism with Lehrman," he wrote.

The picture was completed in three days. Despite Lehrman, Charlie had slipped in comic bits, directing himself, only to see his brilliance vanish from the final print. Years later, Lehrman confessed that he had cut them to get back at the annoying little Cockney.

Committed to acting in two short films a week, Charlie made no secret that he hoped to be spared Lehrman again. But Sennett prevailed. Chaplin and the director were to run out to the beach town of Venice, about twenty-two miles west, where kids were holding a small car race. Keystone was in the habit of stealing events as background action, free of charge.

Chaplin walked into the costume room, and out came the Little Tramp.

He wrote, "I wanted everything a contradiction: the pants baggy, the coat tight, the hat small and the shoes large . . . Remembering Sennett had expected me to be a much older man, I added a small mustache . . ."

And then, "I had no idea of the character. But the moment I was dressed, the clothes and the make-up made me feel the person he was. I began to know him, and by the time I walked onto the stage he was fully born."

Charlie searched out Sennett and gave the tramp a tryout. "I assumed the character and strutted about, swinging my cane."

Sennett, whom Chaplin credits with the golden gift of enthusiasm, all but fell apart with laughter and approval. Chaplin quickly began to fix the character, never forgetting, "Even the clown has his rational moments."

"A tramp, a gentleman, a poet, a dreamer, a lonely fellow . . . He would have you believe he is a . . . musician, a duke, a polo player. However, he is not above picking up cigarette butts or robbing a baby of its candy . . . he will kick a lady in the rear—but only in extreme anger!"

In a matter of moments,
rummaging around in the
Keystone costume room,
Charlie transformed himself
from this . . .

. . . to this.

In shorthand, "His club consists of the sidewalk, his haberdashery, the ashcan."

A banana peel to slip on into a pratfall may be the original comedy prop. In Chaplin's case, his first gadgets were the bowler hat, the patched shoes, and the short toothbrush of a mustache cut out of black crepe. They conspired to make him immortal.

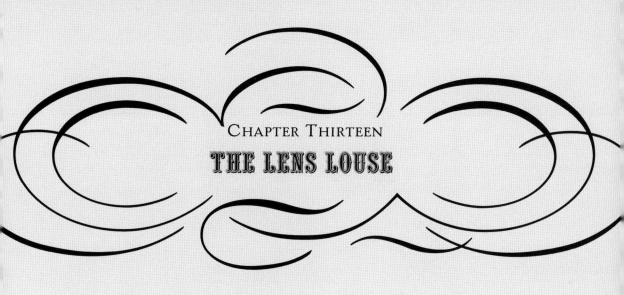

Chapter Thirteen
THE LENS LOUSE

ON THE DRIVE TO THE BEACH, ACTOR AND director agreed on the premise to insinuate Keystone into the race. Lehrman would be directing a cameraman shooting the event. Charlie would play a lens louse. That is to say, he would be a spectator vainly trying to get his face in the lens and the movie. It worked.

Every time the director moved the setup, in shuffles the tramp to mug for the camera. Soon Charlie is almost run down by racing cars, only to duck a cop policing the crowd. He goes from improvisation to inspiration until the cameraman delivers a swift kick to launch him out of the shot and the picture. Charlie dusts himself off, approaches the camera for an angry close-up, and sticks his tongue out at Lehrman to end the newsreel.

The sequence is believed to have taken a mere forty-five minutes to shoot. It ran much less than half a reel: hardly four minutes. To bulk up the length, Chaplin was paired with an educational trip through an olive factory.

Keystone didn't realize what it had, and Chaplin was lucky to get top billing over the olives. Then orders for film prints came in. Audiences had never seen anyone like Chaplin before. They were laughing, and wanted to see more of the knockabout little fellow with the big shoes, little mustache, and soulful eyes.

The Little Tramp had shuffled onto the world stage as if freshly arrived from outer space.

Chapter Fourteen

MABEL, THE MOVIE STAR

IT WAS WARFARE BEHIND THE CAMERA, AND Charlie couldn't bring himself to surrender his comedy instinct. He had a mousetrap mind for catching visual metaphors around him. A tennis racket could be held like a banjo and strummed. After dipping his hands in a finger bowl, he formally wiped them on the hanging beard of the man seated next to him. A pawnbroker examines an alarm clock with a stethoscope as if it were a patient with a bad ticker.

He managed to escape Lehrman only to fall into the lion's jaws of a veteran of hand-cranked movies, Pop Nichols. After Charlie's first offer of an idea, Nichols put an end to such nonsense. Fixing his actor with a frozen glance, he said, "I've been in this business over ten years. What the hell do you know about it?"

Nichols would hardly have a toehold among the footnotes of early Hollywood but for the fluke that he once directed Charlie Chaplin.

It was Charlie rather than his directors who soon picked up the backstage chill of being hard to work with.

He saw at once that the only way he could survive intact in pictures was to direct his own films. He approached Sennett, who regarded it as a crazy notion. What did Charlie know about placing the camera and film cutting and all the inside skills of moviemaking?

Crazy? That was not a word Charlie felt comfortable tossing around. The haunting shadow of the asylum had clung to him since early childhood. Was he tainted? Had he inherited that awful doom from his mother? And his grandmother, too, had been institutionalized for insanity. Throughout his life he was aware of "the specter of nervous breakdown . . . threatening," he wrote, and knocked wood.

No, this new ambition was as sane as the directors he'd been dealing with—although that was far from reassuring. There were times he did feel that at Keystone he was, indeed, in a padded cell with the inmates in charge.

He had kept his eyes open on the set and was a quick study. And a compulsive scholar. He had even begun studying French with Keystone's lovely and clownish star, Mabel Normand. He figured he knew *beaucoup* about filmmaking. He was ready to direct.

Mabel, the movie heartthrob of the day, was an accomplished pantomime actress who was going to launch her own first film. She liked Charlie and cast him as the villain in *Mabel at the Wheel.*

The company was scheduled for location shooting in the suburbs. Almost at once, Charlie and Mabel ran into creative barbed wire. He felt that a certain comedy bit with a bulky garden hose should be added to a scene where Mabel the Actress was wetting down the road, causing the villain's car to skid. Mabel the Director disagreed.

"We have no time!" she protested. "We have no time! Do what you're told."

Steam shot out of Charlie's nose. Said he, "Miss Normand, I will not do what I'm told. I don't think you are competent to tell me what to do."

He walked to the curb and sat down. Everyone on the set wanted to club him for talking so rudely to sweet, charming, twenty-year-old Mabel.

She decided she could not deal with the Cockney's

Mack Sennett and his comedy star, Mabel Normand, all dressed up to sign a new contract. They had never heard of Charlie Chaplin when this 1913 picture was taken. A year would pass before the three show-people bumped into one another's careers.

insubordination, and she directed the company to shut down and return to the studio.

Charlie knew he would be fired. Well, he carried $1,500 in his money belt. That would more than pay his boat fare back to England.

In Edendale, when he was taking off his makeup, in walked Mack Sennett, bristling.

"Do what you're told or get out."

As everyone on film row knew, Mabel was Sennett's inamorata. The producer left without another word, making sure to slam the door.

Charlie pulled off his false mustache. C'est la vie, he thought.

Since he had a contract, he hopped the streetcar for work as usual the next morning.

He was in for a rimshot surprise.

Sennett greeted him with a smile so warm it would have melted candle wax. Wouldn't Charlie swallow his pride and help young Mabel out?

Charlie melted somewhat, too. He'd be good if Sennett would allow him to direct his next picture.

Sennett balked. Who would cover the loss if the film were a disaster?

Charlie said he would. He had $1,500 he'd put up as a guarantee.

Sennett was now beaming like buttered sunshine. They shook on it, and Charlie applied his makeup again.

It was months later that Charlie discovered what had so suddenly warmed Sennett's affections. Overnight, he had received a command from his bosses in the East. The little guy with the funny walk and funny mustache was a smash hit. The producer was to rush new movies without delay.

CHAPTER FIFTEEN

OPUS ONE: THE SLEEPWALKER

ACK SENNETT DID NOT BELIEVE IN RETAKES. The actors got one take before the camera. The first shot became the last shot. And in Keystone's clam-tight economies, a director was allowed ten camera setups or positions for each one-reel comedy. It was moviemaking on the cheap. Later, Chaplin would cavalierly dismiss this bookkeeper's guide to filmmaking. He became notorious for shooting takes by the bucketful in order to achieve what he was after.

But for his first entirely solo performance, he promised to be good and honor the studio culture. Sennett would allow him a maximum thousand-dollar budget. Charlie would be efficient. Dreaming up his own comic drama, he made use of the nearby park, free of charge, and a standing hotel set on the Keystone lot.

There's no evidence that he ever wrote out a script during these years. In the Keystone way, he came up with a story premise and worked out scenes and bits in his head on his solitary streetcar rides home. The rest he improvised under fire.

Later, he would famously confess that all he needed to make a film was "a park, a policeman, and a pretty girl."

Chaplin admitted to a certain panic when he faced his first scene in the park. Where should he place the camera? Lower? Closer? Once he heard his baggy-pants character give the command to start the action, he was committed and his jangle of nerves smoothed out.

It was 1914. He would reprise bits of his tipsy behavior from vaudeville. Centered in a hotel interior, *Caught in the Rain* became a sort of showery bedroom farce. To reach his room, the tipsy gent must climb a flight of stairs. In his entire film career, Chaplin never passed stairs he couldn't slip down. He directed himself on the ascent as if the wooden flight were the snowy Alps. Only seconds long, as Charlie trips and slips and slides, the bit remains a gem of physical comedy.

The plot quickly thickens. A rather bulky woman, with whom the fellow has flirted, is a sleepwalker. She strolls sound asleep into his room. About to be discovered there by her big beef of a husband,

Once Chaplin became accustomed to creating for the camera, he famously remarked that all he needed to make a movie was a park, a cop, and a girl. He proved it in 1915 when he made *In the Park* with a park, a cop, and a girl.

she kicks Charlie through the window to hide outside in the rain. Below, a policeman takes him for a burglar and shoots, forcing him back into the presence of the furious husband for a slapstick fight.

Other Keystone directors were in the habit of shoring up their frenzied dramas with screen dialogue and often with hasty puns in search of a guffaw or two. For example, for footage of a dancing girl in a cabaret, this dialogue card flashed on during an earlier Keystone silent: THE SPEARMINT MOVEMENT,—VERY WRIGLEY . . .

Charlie, the newcomer, quickly trashed such trash. He allowed his story to unfold without the full stops of dialogue to be read. He put his chips on movement and gesture alone. And he worked to a somewhat less manic metronome.

When inspiration failed him, he was apt to break into a jig or clog dance to relax and bemuse his cast and crew. When an idea struck, the *click-click-click* of the camera would resume.

So consumed was he in creating the film that he always seemed to be underfoot. Wrote Sennett, "He wanted to work—and nearly all the time. We went to work at eight o'clock and he'd be there at seven. We'll quit at five . . . but he'd still be around at six."

When he saw the finished film, Sennett was surprised and impressed with Chaplin's quick grasp of directing. He bountifully added a $25 bonus to his salary when Charlie both created the story and directed.

Charlie would never have admitted to Sennett that the producer's earlier judgment hadn't been so far off. What did Charlie know about directing? Only how not to do it. He'd been tutored by primitives. Making this film had reassured him of his unique gift. "It is pure instinct with me—dramatic instinct. I don't figure it out; I just know it is right or wrong." His relationship with Sennett lost its raspy edges and warmed to the familial. They went to dinner together almost every night.

There, with Mabel at the table, they would talk story and bits of business for other Keystone films. Now Charlie's ideas were sought and taken. He could isolate the moments of human nature made comic in the sleepwalker scene when the wife, snoring away, goes through the tramp's pants pockets at night. That had Chaplin's fingerprint: character in the midst of chaos. In addition, as overlay, the tramp could dodge punches and deliver rear-end kicks with the best of them.

He had already developed into a master of motion. His walk was art. Almost every movement was unique to him—like his trademark skid as he turned corners, one leg outstretched. He had a dozen ways of tipping his hat. He showed a ballet dancer's grace in boxing gloves and bare knuckles. When he'd toss away a match or cigarette, it would fly back over his shoulder, there to meet a backward kick and fly off. Audiences waited and roared relentlessly at these trademark Chaplinisms.

That he didn't turn the audience against him when he took a first swing at some brute, as he often did, or delivered kicks to the rear, can be credited to his shortness. His belligerencies come off as pure bravery. He was forever David in a world of Goliaths.

At Keystone, it appeared that the wheel had not yet been invented. Once positioned, cameras didn't budge. They might as well have been set in cement. Charlie had to cavort his actors before the fixed eye of the lens. He couldn't pan anyone into the scene or out. The panning shot, was, as yet, in an embryonic stage.

Despite these limitations, Charlie thrived on both sides of the camera. Said he, "There was a lot Keystone taught me and a lot I taught Keystone."

Charlie brought to his filmmaking things others on the lot had little if any experience of—English pantomime with its emphasis on naturalness, Karno stagecraft, and physical comedy as a form of dance. He even taught some of the stunt comedians how to take falls as he did, without breaking his neck.

As an actor he had to learn not to look at the camera. As a director, he had to know right from left. If he told a character to exit the scene to the right, the actor must enter the next scene from the left. Master that, and you graduate.

Chaplin soon detected the art and hazards of the camera's location. A long shot could make or break an effect. A close-up could jar and kill a scene. Camera placement, he concluded, was style on tripods.

His artist's life was held in the tiring hand of the cameraman, for their equipment was motorless. The photographer needed a steady wrist to crank the film smoothly at sixteen frames per second. Faster, and the screen action would drag into slow motion. If he cranked more leisurely, the fight or chase would race frantically. This cheated reality, a ploy that directors often slipped in, like aces from their sleeves, for comedic effect.

Charlie took it all in with delight. "I was entering a rich, unexplored field. I suppose that was the most exciting period of my career."

CHAPTER SIXTEEN

CHARLIE AND THE TEN-GRAND RUMOR

THE YEAR 1914 BROUGHT WITH IT BLOOD-drenched events performed for the history books. In August, the nations of Europe would indulge their century's old irritations and go to war. Way off in Hollywood, social history failed to make more than a smudged footnote when the first feature-length comedy movie was made. It was called *Tillie's Punctured Romance*, and Charlie was the leading man, if you could call a charming swindler and fortune hunter a leading man.

Only Chaplin, it seemed, could play a villain without losing audience sympathy. How can you hiss a villain who makes you laugh? The film was a monster hit.

Charlie persuaded Sennett to lure the stage-wise Sydney from London. The producer offered the older Chaplin, sight unseen,

$200 a week for a year's contract—somewhat more than he was paying Charlie. But the Little Tramp was prepared to pull a rabbit out of his bowler hat.

His several films for Keystone had been successful. The actor/writer/director's contract would be coming up for renewal. Charlie asked for a thousand dollars a week. More than twenty thousand in today's dollars.

Sennett was almost struck dumb. "But *I* don't make that," he protested.

Chaplin reminded him that it wasn't Sennett's name that jammed the theaters. It was Charlie's.

Shrewdly, Sennett would let his star comedian worry and stew for a while, for what other studio would come across with that kind of money? Charlie would be chastised and scared.

Sennett was right—at first.

Then a mad rumor arose that the Little Tramp was asking for a $10,000 bonus for signing a new contract.

Behold! Along came a cowboy star, Broncho Billy, and a money-tight partner named George Spoor, making pictures as Essanay, eager to sign Charlie.

The comedian, aware of the absurd rumor, kept his mouth shut.

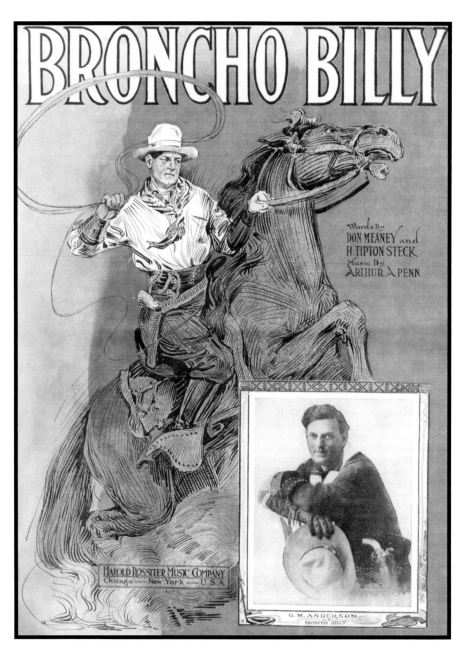

The first of the cowboy stars, Broncho Billy, may not have been entirely literate. He managed to widely publicize but strangely misspell his own movie name—"bronco" is officially spelled without an "h," in its original Spanish and everywhere else. Here's the saddle hero in poster art for a piece of unlamented sheet music.

When Broncho Billy opened his, it was to say, "The deal's on . . . and you get your ten thousand dollars tomorrow."

Now it was Charlie's turn to be struck dumb. He managed to nod an agreement. He didn't need a dialogue card.

Through the decades, that old money rumor has been allowed to float free of suspicion and go unchecked. How did it start? Or, rather, who hatched it? Why?

How about Mack Sennett himself? Sure. Ten grand would strangle at birth any offer for Charlie's services from a rival studio. Keystone wanted to keep its human slot machine. That the fable backfired and enriched Charlie was fate with a sense of irony.

Did Charlie smell a rat? He left Sennett and the Keystone fun factory without saying good-bye. He slipped away like a conscious-stricken housebreaker making off with the family silver. He caught a train for Chicago, where Essanay had turned a former warehouse on shabby Argyle Street into a studio.

Winter had set in and Charlie missed California the moment he stepped off the train and could see January frost on his breath.

The world, meanwhile, was misdirected from Chaplin's career: World War I was trenching its way across France. England was in the fight. Schools of German submarines were in the Atlantic Ocean, spawning torpedoes.

Before Sydney had left London, Charlie worried about being able to get funds past the submarines to their mother for expenses. Late in 1912, they had moved Hannah to a nursing home. Sydney was not always timely in making the weekly payments of a handful of shillings, but he was reliable. Presumably he arranged for long-term care before making the crossing himself. At Keystone, in due time, he replaced Charlie as a moneymaker.

The studio system at Essanay was guaranteed to earn Charlie's scorn. Pictures were made one a week on a sort of assembly line, like Model T Fords. A young woman dealt out scenarios "like playing cards every Monday morning."

When a scenario was offered him, Charlie rejected it as if he were being offered the measles. "I don't use other people's scripts, I write my own," he snapped.

He immediately started rehearsals for a film of his own, prophetically titled *His New Job*. He had to replace a pretty actress named Gloria, whom the studio had signed but who was stiff and unresponsive in the comic scenes. She claimed later that she acted like a wooden board on purpose because she wanted dramatic roles, not slapstick. Hmmm. She went west to work at Keystone, where Gloria Swanson became a star as a comedian in slapsticks.

George Spoor, Charlie's boss in Chicago, was appalled to see his star not only lavish time on his shots, but, horror of horrors—doing retakes.

Charlie requested that Spoor, the S in Essanay, ship him back to California. There, amid the alfalfa fields in Niles, east of San Francisco, the company had a studio with a glass roof for sunlight.

It was there that Broncho Billy Anderson, the first of the cowboy heroes, made his popular one-reel, thousand-foot sagebrush epics. The raw film cost four cents a foot; the company sold the celluloid Westerns for eight to twelve cents a foot. Broncho Billy shot more than 350 of these horseback chase operas, quite possibly on the same horse.

Essanay was able to sell Chaplin films at twenty-five cents a foot while the number of orders skyrocketed. Spoor was eager to keep the demanding little tramp happy, and bought him a train ticket back to the Pacific Ocean.

Charlie brought with him a wildly cross-eyed sidekick regarded as the funniest of his lifelong company of comedy actors. He was a New Orleans native and burlesque comedian named Ben Turpin, handsomely described as "a wizened little man rather like a prematurely hatched bird."

Chaplin's first problem at the Niles studio was to find a leading lady both cinematic and flexible enough for comedy. After a tedious search, he followed up on a tip that led to San Francisco and a blonde from Lovelock, Nevada. She had a quirky name: Edna Purviance (pronounced PurvEYEance).

He'd give her a try, testing her out at a party the night before shooting was to begin. A $10 bet was put up that like Svengali, he could hypnotize her. He fluttered his fingers and gazed into her eyes, but she was no suggestible Trilby. He slipped her a stage whisper to play along. She took the cue and swooned into a performance that Svengali himself would have applauded.

Like Charlie, nineteen-year-old Edna had been abandoned as a child by an uncaring father. Chaplin cared. She had a figure like a Greek statue, but better arms. Before long, a serious romance was evident on both sides of the camera. Though he hated to write letters, he was soon composing billets-doux, hailing Purviance as his own darling Edna.

She acted as his leading lady during the next eight years of his picture making.

Chaplin transformed Edna Purviance, an inexperienced actress from Lovelock, Nevada, into a star in many of his films, including this 1918 smash hit *Shoulder Arms*.

CHAPTER SEVENTEEN
CHARLIE AND THE CROSS-EYED MAN

IT WAS HARD ENOUGH MAKING FILMS WITH intuition for a script, mad perfection for a director, and interior shots taking place on a stage with a glass roof. When the sun was out, and it usually was, the radiant heat was so hot an actor's icy stare was in danger of bursting into flames.

Charlie managed to fill a two-reeler with a rapid fire of visual bits. In *A Night Out*, he and Ben Turpin do a double act as two tipsy chaps with a single premise: trying to stay vertical in a war with gravity. That's all the plot that exists in the first half of the film, and it's enough.

Turpin holds his own against Chaplin's smothering presence. It is only in midfilm that Chaplin solos and a dramatic plot arises, with comic ornamentation. In the hotel, he mistakes the lobby desk for a bar. He tries to hang his foot on the nonexistent bar rail. He helps himself to a drink, only to discover that it is the desk ink. He puts his foot into a cuspidor. In his room, he repeatedly attempts to hang his pants on the wall; they repeatedly slip to the floor. A dog enters with a lady's slipper, quickly followed by the lady herself, followed by her husband. A plot, somewhat warmed over, arrives at last.

By this time the relationship between Chaplin and Turpin was growing thorns. Turpin regarded his director as an English snob and a pest, telling the cross-eyed actor what to do in front of the camera. Chaplin regarded his second banana as lowbrow, coarse, and lacking in dedication to his own art. In addition, Turpin was drawing entirely too much applause and approval from the public. Chaplin was getting jealous. They would soon part.

Turpin hooked up with Keystone. He developed marquee lights, but never with the wattage of his former film sidekick.

Charlie had made four films in Niles when his patience with the place ran out. There was almost no pool of talent to draw from. And he could draw little inspiration from the scent of alfalfa.

For his own reasons, Broncho Billy agreed to let Charlie move south, to Essanay's studio in low-rent Boyle Heights, the Jewish

Ben Turpin insured his crossed eyes for $25,000. He lived in fear that they would straighten themselves and cost him his movie career.

section of Los Angeles. Before long, Sydney's contract with Keystone expired, and he took over as Charlie's business manager.

And Hannah, left behind in London? Peckham House, the nursing home, threatened to send her back to the asylum because of payments in arrears. Had the sons, in the frenetic pace of their lives, overlooked her bills? Or was it the war? Hannah's younger sister, Kate, borrowed money to maintain the patient in the nursing home.

But what about Chaplin's disappeared half-brother, Hannah's youngest son, Wheeler Dryden? Charlie, then a four-year-old, barely remembered the sibling when the boy's father vanished from the family nest, taking his infant son with him into the unknown.

Decades would pass before Wheeler reappeared. Charlie's migratory fame reached the Far East, where the lost brother was working as a small-time comedian. From Singapore, he wrote both Charlie and Sydney to encourage a reconciliation.

In a stroke of filial indifference, neither Charlie nor Sydney bothered to reply. Curious! Did they regard the Singapore man an imposter? If it truly was Wheeler, what was he after? A bite of Charlie's ever-fattening bankroll? Or was there simply no room for an invader in their tight brotherhood? For a reunion, if there was to be one, Wheeler would have to wait in the monsoon rains of Singapore.

Despite studio changes and upheavals, Charlie was energetically productive in 1915. He had begun to earn a bonus of $10,000 for every film he made. Toward the end of the year, he shot his burlesque version of the opera *Carmen*. Edna Purviance became the gypsy spitfire, while he cast himself as the lovesick Spanish Captain of the Guards in slapstick pursuit of her. In the end he tragically stabs Carmen and himself, only to rise with her, giggling, after a tender and weepy death scene. He reveals the secret of their resurrection—a prop dagger. See? It was only a movie.

Once the film was released, Charlie's contract with Essanay expired. He refused to sign a new deal despite an offer of $350,000. Soon after, he discovered Spoor engineering a swindle, well under way.

In the cutting room, Essanay had contrived to stretch the short two-reeler into a one-hour *Carmen* by stitching in Charlie's out-takes, his rejects, and even by shooting a few new scenes.

Charlie exploded. Instead of going after his friend Broncho Billy and the evil Spoor with a dagger—a real one—he went after a lawyer and sued to protect his artistic integrity.

He lost.

On his next contracts, Chaplin grimly added a clause that was unique in Hollywood. Only Charlie could cut, add to, or alter his films. Everyone else: Keep their bloody hands off.

A few years later Essanay went bust and Broncho Billy rode off into the sunset. But Chaplin had come out of his year with a plum.

In a frenzied career of filmmaking (almost forty shorts), he had been unable to get a handle on his alter ego. The character lacked definition—who the heck was the little fellow? Where was he going? At Essanay in 1915 he shot a movie called *The Tramp* and gazed into his mirror image as if for the first time. So that's who his other self was—a tramp! A shuffling prince of the road! A flirtatious rogue. A tramp.

Unlike Chaplin himself, the vagabond's birth was recorded and named. Thereafter, he became known formally as the Little Tramp. But he was otherwise just Charlie. Or Charlot in France. Carlo in Italy. And the more huggable Carlitos in the Spanish-speaking world.

Charlie didn't fully grasp how famous and fabled he'd become until he was making a five-day train trip to New York to meet with Sydney. Traveling without his movie makeup was an easy way of going incognito, for no one recognized him. He was in his shorts, shaving, when the train pulled into Amarillo, Texas. An immense crowd jammed the station. He assumed they had come to welcome some local hero. Then he heard a chant, "Where is he? Where's Charlie Chaplin!"

His telegram to Sydney had been ogled by the operator, who had flashed the news along the wire that the great Charlie would be aboard the train. Kansas City, too, was waiting. Chicago, mobbed. New York put Charlie in newspaper headline type: HE'S HERE! What would they think in Kennington, if they could see the slum brat now?

CHAPTER EIGHTEEN

THE MILLIONAIRE TRAMP

CHARLIE'S EARLY FILMS WERE ACTION MOVIES of the day. There were no cars to chase. The moviemakers anticipated the crashes and doomsday explosions of contemporary films, scaled down to parlor mayhem.

One loses count of the bare-fisted punches thrown in a one-reeler. Or trips and pratfalls. Or pushes, slaps, shoves, shakes, and collisions. And the favored coup de grâce of them all—the swift kick to the rear.

Audiences, then as now, loved the social mutiny, especially when authority was at the receiving end. Laughter was rebellion in Sunday clothes. The nickelodeons were favored by immigrants and the unread, who needed no dialogue to follow what Charlie was up to when he lifted a wooden mallet and gave the villain a sudden headache.

Films were considered so lowbrow that Broadway actors declined to step before the movie camera. Regular theatergoers, too, regarded going to the movies as slumming.

But that would change. And so would Charlie.

Despite the phenomenon of their success—think *Harry Potter*—Charlie's earliest films were largely apprentice work done under the coarse tutelage of Sennett. Despite Essanay and its time-clock philosophy of art, he took extra pains and reshot scenes, littering the cutting-room floor with outtakes.

In 1916, Chaplin moved his cameras to Mutual, a Wall Street–backed production company that was prepared to risk $1.5 million on the Little Tramp. Chaplin would be paid at the rate of $10,000 a week, plus a huge bonus. This pirate's treasure would pin Charlie down to a contract for a year's films. The comic was glad to oblige. Sign here.

Neither the public nor Mutual seemed to mind that Chaplin was a capricious dramatist. It was not often that one detected in his films a whole plot with a beginning, a middle, and an end.

He'd done fifty or so comedies, most balanced as delicately

as a toe dancer on a fragmentary story premise—Charlie as a prehistoric man, a dentist's assistant, a fireman, a scrawny boxer. That was enough to prod his gift for improv.

He was a master of riffs. Start a bare-knuckle fight, and he'd spin pirouettes and duck blows with the timing of a piston. Hang a sword on his hip, and he'd be bound to swing around and strike ladies' corseted derrieres. Put a tub of water in a scene, and everyone but the audience would get an impromptu baptism. Give him a grand prop, such as a department-store escalator, and he'd play it like a Stradivarius.

In only a few of these pioneering Chaplins do the stories end. Most just stop. It's as if the cameraman had run out of film. Charlie evidently felt no need for the dramatist's third-act curtain.

And yet, in *The Tramp*, he shot one of the most memorable curtains in films. The action finished, the vagabond walks down a lonely road to an unknown but hopeful future. The scene has pathos, an emotion he would embrace constantly in his films, setting them apart from movies of the other laugh makers. He had, after all, majored in pathos as a child.

He recognized his own creative freshness and emotional depth and would use these skills again. And again. After lessons learned at Keystone, with its tradition of retreading good scenes like used tires, he filmed the poignant ending effectively again in his 1936 full-length masterpiece, *Modern Times*.

His year with Mutual was happy, for no one interfered with his work or hurried him along. The Mutual comedies have a finer, hand-rubbed finish, and behold! *The Vagabond* has a plot as complete as any Greek dramatist could wish. Here, Charlie unfolds a love story, unhurried, with genuine tenderness. He also plays the left-handed violin.

And for mayhem turned into roughhouse comic art, nothing has bested *Easy Street*. With endless invention, Charlie plays little David to a six-foot-four Goliath with a scowl that would stop a charging moose.

By this time the Tramp was so widely mimicked that a holdup man in Cincinnati impersonated the film star to shuffle into a bank and rob it.

The real Charlie lived the life of a quiet and preoccupied young bachelor in two rooms at the Los Angeles Athletic Club. After a day's filmmaking, he usually had dinner in the club and settled down to an evening's reading or a long, solitary walk.

Chaplin's huge utility villain, with black eyebrows like the wings of a crow taking flight, was Eric Campbell, an actor from Scotland. Here, Charlie as a policeman captures the mammoth bully of *Easy Street* (1917), with the help of a street gaslight earlier bent by the villain himself.

The war was still alive, and more than once the symbolic white feather of cowardice was floated for his failure to serve in uniform. The British government was sorry to deny him the opportunity to die in the mud trenches of France. He would be of more service to his country making films and keeping laughter alive. Anyway, the army didn't have uniforms small enough to fit him.

One Sunday he was invited to a swimming party at the beach home of film producer Sam Goldwyn. Had Charlie the slightest intuition that the evening would alter his life, he would have dodged the invitation.

There a former child actress, grown up blonde and starstruck, would improvise a campaign to catch the catch of Hollywood. Her name was Mildred Harris. They met. He gave her an impromptu lift home. Once returned to the athletic club, he banished her from his mind.

At the same time, an ambitious dream waiting its moment was quickly turning to brick and mortar. At age twenty-seven, the penniless tramp had made Chaplin a millionaire. He was tired of bosses, even of his benign bondage to Mutual. He turned away from its checkbook, refusing to renew the accompanying contract.

Charlie left his footprints in cement on a studio step, inscribing his name and the year 1918.

The English cottage—style buildings of the original Chaplin Studio survive.

Instead, in 1917, he began building a studio of his own. His next contract would be with himself.

He had chosen a five-acre plot of orange and lemon trees in an upscale residential fringe at Sunset Boulevard and La Brea. His moneyed neighbors were suffering cardiac episodes that a film company, with its disreputable actors and shantytown buildings, was soon to squat in their midst.

Chaplin, stepping out of his chauffeur-driven twelve-cylinder blue Locomobile, chilled their fears with renderings of the sedate and sturdy English bungalows about to go up. Charlie dug into his pocket for $35,000, and in three months he had a state-of-the-art studio with film lab and cutting room. The cement still wet outside the entry, there he impaled his splayed footprints, as unique as his signature. The studio still stands, but in lesser glory.

While the paint was drying, Sydney found money to back eight new comedies. It was time to put the studio facilities to the test.

CHAPTER NINETEEN

DAWN ON SUNSET BOULEVARD

NOT ONLY DID CHARLIE HAVE A CHAUFFEUR, HE acquired a private secretary and an "English" valet who was Japanese. It was not that he needed these gaudy ornaments of wealth. He was discovering that greenbacks deposited in the bank became invisible to the naked eye. One had to be an accountant to distinguish the filthy rich from the filthy poor. Having his own personal staff reassured him that he was no longer penniless.

He had lived frugally despite his early success. Haunted by a prickly fear that the bottom would fall out, he had demanded great sums up front before signing new contracts. One of these days, he feared, his audiences and his bosses would get wise to him. They'd see that he was nothing but a low Cockney comedian putting on airs.

In late 1917, he threw himself into his first independent film for First National, his financial backer. And for the first time he was shooting with two cameras. So many copies were in demand that the single negatives of his earlier films were aging in the heavy printings and losing definition.

The backup negative proved to be valuable insurance. In a year or two, he would make the first of his feature-length masterworks, *The Kid*. And one of its negatives was to vanish in a fire.

In 1918, ready to film *A Dog's Life*, he began the preproduction by combing alleys in a talent search for a dog. From the city pound alone, he screen tested some twenty-one beasts. He had in mind the tramp and a mongrel trying to survive in a mean London slum. The streets of his childhood, say.

He was already having the set built. And, his perfectionism satisfied at last, he had his dog, a clever mutt called Mutt.

But there were great distractions behind the camera. It was early in 1918, and the bloodletting of war overseas was in high tide. The U.S. had now thrown in with the British and the French against the belligerent Germans. Chaplin was asked to interrupt moviemaking to pack and go on a patriotic tour with his close friends, the beloved film stars Douglas Fairbanks and Mary

Drawing immense crowds on a tour to sell government war bonds. Charlie is standing on the shoulders of fellow movie star Douglas Fairbanks.

Pickford. They were to beat the drums for war bonds, needed to finance the fighting.

And Edna?

The girl from Lovelock, Nevada, the great romance of his life, was discovered going out with a handsome leading man from Paramount Studios. Charlie was shaken. He could barely sleep or work.

He pulled himself together. By shooting and cutting for three days, around the clock, he managed to finish *A Dog's Life*, with Edna still the leading lady. After a hard look at low life, the picture segues into a mongrel Rin-Tin-Tin epic with laughs.

Without having to wait for a musical score, the silent was released two weeks later. Commentators crowned the urban epic with an Oscar years before the Academy Awards were invented. "The cinema's first total work of art," said one impassioned critic.

At last, unburdened of film work, Charlie found himself train-bound across the country during the spring of 1918. The three film legends were attracting brass bands and frenetic crowds equal to the population of small cities. The stars' appearances sold war bonds as if they had gone on sale.

Haranguing the Washington crowd, Charlie got so patriotically worked up that he fell off the edge of the bunting-draped platform. There, buffering his fall, stood a tall, handsome young Navy man of destiny who would later become president. He was Franklin D. Roosevelt.

Returning to California, Charlie was unwilling to revive the Charlie/Edna romance: A stake had been driven through its heart. But his old affection ran so deep that in time he was able to give a worldly and forgiving shrug and to keep Edna on for his next film and others to follow. He maintained her on his payroll for the rest of her life. She never married and lived until 1958.

When First National forked over the money to finance his films, he had agreed to hire the best writers available to help with his stories.

Back at his studio still smelling of fresh paint, Charlie was without a story idea. The earlier agreement to bring in literary hired hands evidently slipped his mind—if, indeed, he had ever regarded it as anything but lawyer talk.

He had returned from his trip with a more acute sense of the war fever in the country. Why not a comedy about the war?

Comedy and war? Friends advised him against it. Dangerous stuff!

Charlie kneels with Marie Dressler, his co-star in *Tillie's Punctured Romance*. Douglas Fairbanks and the celluloid heartthrob Mary Pickford stand behind the comedian. To the left, looking straight at the camera, stands Franklin Delano Roosevelt, who would become president of the United States and outshine them all.

Depends, thought he. What if the Little Tramp were in uniform? What if he singlehandedly captured the steel-helmeted German kaiser?

Chaplin loaded up his cameras. *Shoulder Arms* was to be feature length, a five-reeler. The gags were coming. Lice in the trenches so big that Charlie wears a mousetrap to catch them. With lead flying overhead, he holds up a bottle so a bullet can take off the cap. A gift package of Limburger cheese so knock-'em-dead smelly, he uses it as a hand grenade.

Before long, he was running into problems and bafflements. Overhead, even the heavens flashed a cosmic warning. On June 8, 1918, a solar eclipse darkened the West, and Charlie had to interrupt shooting for lack of daylight.

His confidence in the work was developing the blues. He wasn't sure his footage was even funny. He became silent and allowed the cameras to stop clicking. On the set, the actors and crew were picking up the sense of doom.

His blue eyes kept glancing over to the discard bin. He was way over budget and had been able to summon inspiration enough to shoot only three of the projected five reels. His film should be put out of its misery.

Charlie asked his friend Fairbanks, dashing star of *Robin Hood* and

Chaplin ready for war, fitted out with a mousetrap to catch large trench lice in *Shoulder Arms* (1918).

Charlie's brother Sydney played the imperial German kaiser, whom the private, fresh from the trenches, captures unaided.

other tales of adventure, to have a look and confirm his judgment.

Fairbanks obliged by lifting the roof with booms of laughter. Charlie in the trenches, lighting a cigarette from another flying bullet? Ambling closer to the enemy while camouflaged as a migrating tree? Capturing the German kaiser (played to perfection by Sydney)?

Fairbanks couldn't believe that Charlie had been mad enough to consider junking the film. The trench scenes were hilarious. If anyone doubted that Chaplin, as widely advertised, was the funniest man in the world, this would remove all doubt.

The ugly duckling of a movie became a smash hit. Soldiers from the real trenches laughed it up.

And then, much to his own surprise, Charlie got married.

CHAPTER TWENTY

A MARRIAGE OF MAYFLIES

MILDRED HARRIS WAS A SEVENTEEN-YEAR-OLD actress with a shapely foot on the lowest rung of the cinematic ladder. After Charlie had driven her home from the Sam Goldwyn beach party, she cast the telephone in the role of winged cupid in her bold pursuit of romance. Her cunning had been adolescent in maneuvering Charlie into driving her home, but after all he was the most famous bachelor in town—and, at a mere twenty-nine, the richest. She was crazy to become a famous player on the movie scene, a blond satellite to Chaplin's fixed star in the Hollywood sky. She lifted the phone.

After dialing the Athletic Club and posting a message, she left herself to the hazards of chance.

Remembering the starstruck actress at the beach party, Charlie

Mildred Harris, a seventeen-year-old actress, trapped the rich and famous Chaplin into a shot-gun marriage when she told the twenty-nine-year-old comedian that she was pregnant. It was a cunning and immortal matrimonial plot—she wasn't expecting anything but a million-dollar settlement when the marriage ended.

phoned back. He was pleased to take her out and see her again, and be seen with her. After several dates, she asked him if he would ever marry. "Never," he replied emphatically. His stock answer. He was accustomed to being pursued by women.

In his autobiography, he treats the romance as if they had had the life expectancies of mayflies. A marriage proposal was sudden and impulsive. The day was quickly set. The informal ceremony took no longer than tying one's shoelaces. Voilà! They were hitched.

It appears to have been a perfect piece of stagecraft on the part of the bride. The romance soon showed the powder burns of a shotgun marriage.

She had confided to Charlie that she was pregnant. He was too famous and beloved to survive a scandal. The newspapers would shred him. He'd be ruined. He had had no option but to instantly make an honest woman of her, and a gentleman of himself.

With rice still in their hair, they moved to a suitable mansion at 2000 De Mille Drive in North Hollywood, there to be unhappy in comfort.

And there to discover that she wasn't pregnant at all.

With English reserve, Chaplin has written nothing of his private groans at being blindsided into wedded bliss. And how embarrassing to be drawn into the oldest shell game in the history of matrimony. "I had been caught in the mesh of a foolish circumstance," he wrote.

She was, after all, lovely to look at. "Although I was not in love," he added nobly, "now that I was married I wanted to be and wanted the marriage to be a success."

He was struck to discover that her mind was distracted and untouchable. "It was cluttered with pink-ribboned foolishness." She regarded the marriage to be "as thrilling as winning a beauty contest." Further, he added, "She was in a continual state of dazzlement."

The curtain fell on their cardboard romance when, at the end of a year, a true pregnancy resulted in a child, a son, who survived only three days. Charlie was genuinely crushed and disabled for work by the event. This was a cruel and heartless pratfall delivered by real life.

Mildred now found her celebrity spouse to be moody, silent, and with his nose forever in Macaulay's endless *History of England*. She felt bored and ignored and invisible, especially when he was preoccupied with a film.

Privately, both were thinking of a friendly divorce. He would write her a check for $100,000 in 1920 dollars. Distraction and heartbreak laid to rest, Charlie eagerly moved back to the Athletic Club and gave full concentration to his next project, whatever it might prove to be.

And then Mildred—possibly taking her cues from Chaplin's money men, First National, who were in a dispute of their own with him—changed her mind.

And asked for a million dollars.

CHAPTER TWENTY-ONE
WHERE'S CHARLIE?

CUSTARD PIES WERE FLYING. BEHIND THE SCENES, Hollywood was in a fracas. The production corporations and theater owners were conspiring to merge and corner the entire business, freezing out the pesky independents.

The conspirators had not counted on the creative heavy hitters and Hollywood elite. Chaplin, Fairbanks, and Pickford met with cowboy star William S. Hart and megadirector D.W. Griffith. They would counter with an independent merger of their own. They formed United Artists to make and distribute their own films.

The upstart plan not only made headlines, it made movie history. United Artists went its own independent way for decades. It has faded but still functions, lacking only its early giants.

Independent spirits fought the major studios trying to corner the film world by forming their own company, United Artists. On the left sit movie megastars Douglas Fairbanks and Mary Pickford. At the right, the fabled director D. W. Griffith.

Jackie Coogan, age six and a half, was the wonder kid of Chaplin's 1921 masterpiece *The Kid*, and became the first of the great child movie stars. Authority is the villain to be ever eluded, including in this posed still.

Charlie had long harbored the notion of shooting a feature film. One- and two-reelers demanded the economy of sonnets. A feature gave a director the novelist's gift of space and leisure—and story. He was bored with stringing gags together like sausages. A feature would offer room for shadows and the other side of comedy, sorrow and tragedy.

It was 1919 before the right story popped up.

It just happened that Charlie had caught the current vaudeville show at the Orpheum Theatre in downtown Los Angeles. It just happened that a four-year-old footlight prodigy was on the bill with his father. The boy's name was Jackie Coogan. He could dance, mimic, and charm like nobody's business. Well, perhaps like Charlie himself so long ago.

Finally, it just happened that Chaplin's old Keystone costar, Fatty Arbuckle, had caught the act, too, and pinned the kid to an informal agreement.

Chaplin was galvanized into action. He had no film in mind, but he wasn't going to let that knee-high bundle of talent get away. He outflanked Arbuckle and hastened to put Coogan in front of a camera. The kid would become a movie star at age six and earn more than all his Irish ancestors combined, going back to the Stone Age.

The *kid.* That would be a natural as a movie title. All Chaplin needed now was a story to prop it up.

Chaplin's way of filming was becoming so spendthrift that he thought nothing of keeping his cast waiting for hours—even days—while he searched the darkness for ideas. On one occasion he vanished for six days in pursuit of the unknown.

His studio was regarded as "a royal court headed by an absolute monarch." He was known to command that a set be built with no story in mind. If an idea didn't spring forth, he would strike—dismantle—the set.

Instead of doing rough drafts with typewriter and paper to give ideas a tryout, he would rewrite with cameras rolling. It was his "rude, untutored genius" at work.

He would commonly shoot cans of film to get a few hundred feet of usable work. But only when he saw a scene flickering by on a screen could he be sure that he'd achieved what he was after. "Even in slapstick, there is an art," he insisted. In movie after movie, he became notorious for regarding each scene as an enigma to be solved only through endless retakes.

As he was handed a fixed sum to make each film, he had to pay the wastage from his own pocket. If he hadn't been working for himself, he would have been fired.

Chapter Twenty-Two
ROOM SERVICE

WHEN CHAPLIN CONFIDED TO A WRITER THAT he was contemplating a film joining slapstick to tragedy, he was advised, in effect, to lie down and take a couple of aspirins. Such a headache of opposites wouldn't work. It was crazy. But isn't that what he'd been warned before shooting his war comedy? And wasn't *Shoulder Arms* a smash hit?

Again he had the confidence to follow his own intuitive hunch.

Crouching between the two cameras, he committed himself with scene one, take one. The film was under way. The Kid would be orphaned, of course, as he himself had been orphaned by the madness of his mother.

The story developed into the first film autobiography. You could see it in the bones. The Kid, abandoned by his mother, quickly falls under the protection of the penniless Tramp—let's say the older, penniless Sydney. They live in a garret room that might as well have adjoined a pickle factory. Surviving by their wits, they bond.

And then there's the gripping scene of the Kid being dragged off to the orphanage/workhouse in what could pass as the rattling bakery van of Chaplin's own past.

But now genius takes over. Veteran of a hundred de rigueur film pursuits, Chaplin filmed the most emotional and unforgettable chase in movie history. The Tramp leaps and flies from rooftop to rooftop as he tearfully attempts to catch up with the truck, to rescue the Kid from the orphanage. If one can watch the sequence without tear ducts overflowing and heart in throat, one needs jumper cables.

This was hardly slapstick. In fact, there are laughs in the film only early on. Discovering an abandoned infant, the Tramp learns that the baby leaks. Cutting a hole in a chair for the tyke, he slips a spittoon under it. He feeds the baby from a teakettle with a nipple over the spout.

During this movie, Chaplin's personal life intruded upon his film work. As in the story, in which the Kid's mother materializes and the two are reunited, Chaplin's mother rematerialized. She was

Chaplin was the first to give comedy a third dimension—pathos. Watching the Kid clinging to the man he regards as his father, movie viewers regularly shed a Niagara of tears.

pronounced sane, and plans were afoot to bring her to California.

Chaplin had no longer remained the attentive son. He had hardly written to Hannah since arriving in the States, if, indeed, he wrote at all. At this point, he sent off a sort of poison-pen cable to Sydney, then in New York.

SECOND THOUGHTS CONSIDER WILL BE BEST MOTHER REMAIN IN ENGLAND SOME GOOD SEASIDE RESORT AFRAID PRESENCE HERE MIGHT DEPRESS AND AFFECT MY WORK

Hannah remained on at Peckham House. Charlie was willing to pay her bills but had no time for emotional revivals.

Now that he was finishing up *The Kid*, Mildred was busy with her lawyers to create the million-dollar divorce. She complained publicly of his remoteness and cheapness and mental cruelty. Some nights he would isolate himself with his violin and play wild tarantellas. Mental cruelty, for sure.

So cheap was he, she publicly revealed, that "she couldn't extract a penny from him with a vacuum cleaner"—a metaphor that sounds suspiciously piped in by her attorney.

Chaplin admitted that he kept her virtually penniless—on a

penurious $50,000 put at her disposal. He had the check stubs to prove it.

Charlie's clairvoyant lawyer had already advised him to get the movie negative out of town before Mildred's lawyers could grab it. In the black hours of an August morning, Charlie's cameraman and assistants concealed the film in coffee cans—twelve crates of them—to board the train to Salt Lake City. Chaplin would meet them at Los Angeles's Union Station, and they would sneak out of town.

He wouldn't be recognized, of course, not without his little mustache and tramp's shoes and bowler hat. He even disguised himself behind dark glasses.

Never underestimate the X-ray eye of a child. A finger pointed and a shout went up. Charlie Chaplin! There he was! A crowd set upon him like a flight of bees. His days of incognito travel were finished.

In adjoining Salt Lake hotel rooms, Charlie and his technicians began cutting the movie. The film cement was hardly dry before he previewed the patchwork in a local theater.

The audience broke into tears and laughter and kept it up for the entire five reels. The tender, comic epic would be an immense hit. Evidently, Chaplin could do no wrong.

In the end, Mildred settled for $200,000 and a toothy bite of community property. A firefly among the stars in the Hollywood sky, she completely faded from sight before long.

Chapter Twenty-Three
THE ETERNAL WASHTUB

WITH *THE KID* FINISHED AND OFF HIS MIND, Charlie's thoughts returned to his mother waiting in London. He hadn't seen her in ten years.

In 1921, he sent his longtime secretary to London to fetch her for the voyage to New York and on to California. She seemed perfectly well until they reached Immigration. The officer was pleased to greet her. "So you're the mother of our famous Charlie."

"Yes," said Mother sweetly, "and you are Jesus Christ."

Was this woman sane enough to be allowed into the United States? Only after Immigration was assured that she would not become a burden on the state was she allowed to enter.

As she stepped down off the cross-country train in Pasadena to avoid a crowd in the Los Angeles station, Charlie was struck to see his vibrant mother recast into "a little old lady."

He and Sydney found her a comfortable seaside bungalow and provided her with caretakers and a car. She was now near enough that they could visit her in the evenings and recharge their old lives together.

She'd have herself driven to the studio, and Charlie would run his movies for her. What she thought of her son as a sore-footed bum along Kennington Road has been recorded. Said she, "If only you had put your talent in the service of the Lord—think of the thousands of souls you could have saved."

Later that year, an exhausted Charlie hopped a grand steamship back to England and Europe, this time as a conquering hero. Visiting the eternal slums of his past, he was recognized on its unkempt streets and followed about like a pied piper. "I have a notion that he suffers from a nostalgia for the slums," wrote the novelist Somerset Maugham, sensing the sadness behind Chaplin's humor.

The returning son was pleased to see one of the monuments to his childhood still standing—the old horse trough where he used to steal a wash. In his films, he could never pass a tub of water without directing someone to pratfall into it. It seemed a payback for his youthful humiliations.

Chaplin was bedazzled by the famous and struck up friendships with notables; here he is with Albert Einstein and the physicist's wife.

The European vacation became an endless game of hide and seek, with his own fame in constant pursuit. As often as not, he had to run for cover—or the nearest taxi. But if others were movie-struck, he was celebrity-struck. *My Trip Abroad*, his book-length account of the trip, is as full of names as a phone book—all celebrities he met and even dined with. He seems to have harbored a sense of wonder to find himself in chummy company with writers H. G. Wells (*War of the Worlds*) and J. M. Barrie (*Peter Pan*), and such world figures as Albert Einstein and Mahatma Gandhi. Imagine! Him, a kid with a lingering Cockney accent.

Home and abroad, he was ever expanding his ambitions as a filmmaker and his coming of age as a citizen. He despised Shakespeare for his preoccupation with kings, queens, princes, and lesser royal fry. "In my pursuit of bread and cheese, honor was seldom trafficked in," he explained. "I cannot identify myself with a prince's problems."

His politics were rooted in his own mean beginnings among the common poor: a leftward and radical tilt that, years later, would come close to destroying him.

But his lone-wolf filmmaking was taking great strides. He felt ready to launch a true epic. About what?

A subject caught his fancy when he was looking at three-dimensional views of Gold Rush Alaska through a stereopticon, a common home entertainment device at the time.

The Gold Rush!

That was all he needed to kick-start his imagination. He began to accumulate ideas for comic scenes. Rubbing noses with an Eskimo maiden—he would have a drippy cold. No, cut that. How about the freezing Donner Party in California eating their moccasins? Yes. Save that. Chased by a polar bear? Of course!

While he was to shoot the epic without a formal script, he had a loose scenario on paper and felt sufficiently scene-ready to begin the picture in early 1924. He had laughs stuffed and waiting up both sleeves. The rest he would improvise, as usual.

Chapter Twenty-Four
DÉJÀ WOES

CHARLIE HAD ORDERED TONS OF COMMON SALT and flour trucked to the studio. This was conjured into a vast snowfield. Across these kitchen breadstuffs the picture began— and so did Charlie's next romance. The movie would be an unforgettable masterpiece. As to the romance and impending new marriage, he gallantly dismissed both, brewing up a demitasse of apologies in his autobiography. His new wife became, after all, the mother of their two sons.

His first impulse was to cast his reliable leading lady, Edna Purviance, as a saloon dancer. He harbored a lingering concern and loyalty toward her and tried to keep her before the camera.

But strong drink had added pounds to her feminine geometry, giving her matronly curves. The extra fullness began a chain of events that led directly to a second marital calamity for Chaplin.

He would have to track down a new leading lady. When a woman with her quiet daughter, Lillita, visited the set, Charlie was shooting a cabin scene on the salt-and-flour snowfield.

It was not the first time Lillita McMurray, now in her teenage years, had seen the famous comedian. Her mother had improvised a meeting in a restaurant when the child was six years old. The girl had won a small part in his work in progress at the time.

The years had filled her out into an attractive, big-boned young lady with dark, cautious eyes. Charlie had a screen test made. His veteran cameraman, Rollie Totheroh, was not impressed. He could find no spark in her. His frowning judgment brought nods around the studio.

Charlie followed his own instinct and signed her as leading lady at $75 a week. She changed her name to Lita Grey.

The troupe then traveled by private railroad car to icy Truckee, California, near Lake Tahoe in the Sierra Nevada mountains. There a second unit had corralled some six hundred derelict men from Sacramento to work as extras. Charlie intended to duplicate the stunning and historic image of gold seekers in single file advancing like black ants through the frozen divide of the Chilkoot Pass.

Lita and her mother, Mrs. Spicer, settled into a room in Truckee's only hotel. A chamber pot was the hotel's only happy concession to modern times.

Mrs. Spicer was there to keep an eye on her daughter, but she must have nodded off in her parka. Lita's relationship with her director was segueing into an off-camera romance.

The company moved back to the studio, where Alaska was reproduced. A mountain rose in days, a feat left to Chaplin's crews rather than the Almighty, who may have frowned at the choice of chicken wire, burlap, and plaster as building materials. For the blizzard scenes, four cartloads of confetti remained offstage, awaiting their cue. There'd be some left over for the unscripted wedding.

Charlie had already shot a scene that would make him famous, if he were not already famous. He and a big miner, Mack Swain, are starving in their cabin. Chaplin boils a hobnailed boot and the two men dine on it with the relish they might bring to a delicate trout. As if he'd found a chicken's wishbone, Charlie hooks his little finger around a bent shoenail and invites his cabin partner to join in making a wish. Meanwhile, he chews down the shoelaces as if they were spaghetti.

The brute, still famished, hallucinates. He sees Charlie as a big,

Charlie signs Lita Grey to a contract as his leading lady in *The Gold Rush* (1925). She doesn't look too happy about her big break, and indeed, was dropped from the picture when she became pregnant. As he had with his first hasty wedding, Chaplin rushed the teenager before a man of the cloth and married her.

Charlie looking for gold, lacking an overcoat in the Alaskan deep freeze. He consults a map and gazes off into the unknown.

A starving Charlie boils and eats his shoes in this classic scene from *The Gold Rush*.

clucking chicken. A flapping chase around the cabin follows, with the hungry man salivating and ready to start carving a wing.

The scene has never been equaled or trumped for its slapstick poignancy.

Chaplin had remained unmarried for the first twenty-nine years of his life. So it is surprising that he would go to so much trouble to retread his recent matrimonial woes. It wasn't that he was a slow learner. He wasn't learning at all.

It had been some six years since Mildred Harris had told him they were expecting a baby.

Now it was Lita's turn. Only her pregnancy was not false. It was the real event.

Charlie shut down the picture. He and Lita rushed off to the Mexican coast to be hastily married among the cacti in Guaymas.

Upon their return, Charlie dropped his expectant bride from the cast of *The Gold Rush* and began the search for a new leading lady. He settled upon Georgia Hale, a former Miss Chicago, who tended a Spanish curl in the middle of her forehead. Her speech was burdened with a light lisp, but that would go unheard in a silent.

The picture resumed production following New Year's Day in 1925. As Chaplin had shot in sequence, he had had to replace

Lacking a leading lady in his Alaskan epic, he cast Georgia Hale, a Chicago beauty-pageant winner.

little of Lita's work, for the leading lady didn't make her entrance until midway though the story.

Charlie had a scene to shoot with a live bear that he found to be more compatible than the young bride he had installed in his home. She was to recall that her presence in the house was less as a bride than as an unwanted guest.

Georgia Hale had an easier time of it on the studio stage. As there was no dialogue to be learned and emoted, there was no need of a script. Charlie told her, as he did all his actors, what to do and exactly how to do it. He was notorious for acting out in advance each part in each scene. "You knew you were working with a genius," she wrote.

Chapter Twenty-Five
Dancing Around the Stake

"Don't eat peanuts or drop shells on the floor."
—Movie title card

LIKE THE KRAKATAU VOLCANO, *THE GOLD RUSH* exploded upon the world with plenty of flash and rumble and a certain amount of dust. The big cities loved it. The *New York Herald Tribune* wrote in 1925, "Chaplin is a genius!"

Small towns at first missed the sausages of gags and trips and pratfalls and kicks to the posterior. This was not entirely the Charlie they had expected to see. At the same time, was there anything funnier than hungry Charlie boiling his shoe for dinner? Or jabbing two forks into dinner rolls and allowing the breadstuffs to dance and high kick a can-can?

Box offices began to overflow with gold. The picture turned around and earned millions. The excitement was in full roar when fatherhood burst in on Charlie. His son Charles Jr. was born.

The infant grew up to write a warm but sharp-eyed autobiography of life with Father. Of the marriage of his parents, he wrote, "It was the torture of complete incompatibility."

The family attempted to exist under one roof in the "stout yellow house on the hill," the Beverly Hills mansion Chaplin had built on Summit Drive in 1923. He had expected to grow roots there. Instead, he grew fangs.

He had bared them from time to time at the studio when someone displeased him. Now it was Lita's turn. She couldn't please him, not even with the gift of a second son, Sydney. Despite his snarling behavior, she cared enough to feel jealous of other women in his professional life—especially his new leading lady. But soon, even this emotion turned to contempt.

Despite her Catholicism, divorce was predictable. The miracle was that the marriage lasted as long as it did—two years. Her divorce complaint took up forty-two pages of poison darts. She accused him of everything but cannibalism.

It became impossible for Chaplin to work. He'd begun preparations for a new comedy about the circus late in 1925. Now he couldn't keep his mind on sawdust clowns and caged beasts. In exhaustion, he'd already had a mild nervous breakdown. Was this a

For all his fame, Chaplin guarded a sense of privacy. When he built his great mansion on Summit Drive in Beverly Hills, he planted young pine trees. They grew up to provide the privacy he sought, but by then he had been driven out of the country by pious gossip and vengeful Washington politicians.

Charlie learned to walk the tightrope for scenes in *The Circus* (1928). To this he added escaped monkeys, to intensify the comedy.

warning of a padded cell waiting to ambush him? He'd threatened to give up filmmaking and return to England.

But soon he was back in his studio, picking up the pieces of *The Circus.* Work was the cure-all and center of gravity of his life. And fame was as demanding as having an exotic pet. It needed to be constantly hand-fed.

He learned to walk a tightrope. He began shooting in January of 1926. But if ever there was a film that contrived not to get made, it was this one.

The entire first month's filming had to be trashed. It was ruined in the laboratory. Charlie developed insomnia and started over again.

The next several months went well until a fire broke out in September. The circus set was completely destroyed. Much of the studio collapsed into a smoking junkyard.

In ten days, with hard-nosed obsession, Chaplin was back shooting around the ashes. It was a temporary reprieve.

The U.S. government padlocked what was left of the studio for taxes unpaid. Charlie owed a cool million. He shut down the picture.

With impeccable bad timing, one more pratfall awaited the Little Tramp. Lita's attorney, her uncle Edwin McMurray, was out for blood. He had an eye on Chaplin's films. For the second time,

Charlie packed up a work in progress—this time, the incomplete circus movie—to shield it from the claws of lawyers.

Newspapers were attentive to the divorce, and public opinion turned heavily against Chaplin. Wrote the public wit H. L. Mencken, "The very morons who worshipped Charlie Chaplin six weeks ago now prepare to dance around the stake while he is burned."

In the end, Chaplin settled the matter with the highest divorce figures on the books—a million dollars, including trust funds of a hundred thousand dollars each to their two sons.

Once his personal winter came to an end, and the government unlocked the studio doors, Charlie quickly finished up *The Circus*. Almost two years had passed coaxing the slapstick drama from its opening shot to its fadeout.

CHAPTER TWENTY-SIX
SILENCE SPOKEN HERE

FOR ALL THE TRAVAIL IN GETTING IT ON FILM, *The Circus* did not make box office history. It was a mere success. Earning back its cost a couple of times over was a piffling return by Chaplin's standards. Still, he had an affection for the opus. He recalled it as "charming."

The sawdust epic is not without its knee-slappers. When Charlie is trying to keep his balance on the high wire, runaway monkeys jump and cling to him. It's nightmare rendered in slapstick. As a grace note, he pulls an inspired variation on the classic comedy prop: a monkey drops a banana peel on the high wire and Charlie slips on it.

Nightmare again when Charlie finds himself in the lion cage, with the lion still in it. This is the scene reputed to have gone

Here, the lion upstages the star in *The Circus*. The lion was the only "actor" to work with Chaplin who didn't later attempt to cash in by writing a book about the comedian.

through two hundred takes. The beast, evidently, did not take direction well. Charlie almost matched the record in a later film, *A Woman of Paris*, making his romantic lead endure a screen kiss some one hundred times. The heroine went through enough lipstick to paint a small house.

Chaplin's infamous passion for retakes is credited to perfectionism. But the lofty numbers suggest other forces at work. In the matter of the kiss, was he punishing Edna Purviance for her old romance with another actor?

How much difference could there have been between shots fifty-seven and ninety-three? In so many other marathon retakes, was a streak of sadism directing the director? The actor Marlon Brando, the leading man in Chaplin's final film, saw the naked meanness up close in Chaplin's humiliations of his actor son Sydney before the cast and crew.

Within a month of *The Circus* and its disappointing box office, Chaplin was at work on a new feature, *City Lights*. This one would prove to be a masterwork, followed by another (*Modern Times*) and another (*The Great Dictator*)—three film classics in a row. And each a box-office bombshell. Never count genius out.

The ink had hardly dried on the million-dollar checks he was writing to Lita Grey and the U.S. government when a different bombshell dropped on Hollywood.

Someone had the impertinence to invent sound, or at least a way to graft it onto movies. In October 1927, Warner Bros. released a modified musical called *The Jazz Singer* during which theatergoers could hear the star, Al Jolson, actually sing. It was a miracle approaching the parting of the Red Sea.

Chaplin, lacking his usual savvy, dismissed sound as a passing nuisance. He had easily adapted the illusion of sound to pantomime in *The Vagabond*: Edna is scrubbing at a washtub. The Little Tramp takes out his fiddle and plays a manically fast Hungarian rhapsody. Edna finds herself trying to keep up, now scrubbing manically fast. All silent.

Chaplin gave sound three years to peak and vanish. At the same time, panic was directing traffic along Hollywood Boulevard. Actors with absurd accents or squeaky voices were shown the exits. Studios were refitting for sound and importing Broadway actors who didn't mumble or who were free of accents.

"They are spoiling the oldest art in the world—the art of pantomime," Chaplin declared. "They are ruining the great beauty of silence."

Chaplin and his mother in Hollywood. When she died, she would be buried among movie stars in a nearby celebrity cemetery.

Nevertheless, he shut down preliminary planning on *City Lights*. If the Little Tramp had to speak, what sounds would come out of his mouth?

Every voice would be the dead wrong voice.

The universal language of Chaplin's alter ego was silence.

In the end, he compromised with himself. He'd put in sound effects and background music, but no spoken dialogue. Absolutely not! *City Lights*, with its leading lady in the role of a blind flower seller, would be essentially a silent film.

Meanwhile, nearby hovered Chaplin's mother, Hannah. He visited her only when he must, for he found that after a visit he would suffer a black depression for a day or two. It was as if their past together had forged itself to a festering memory.

It is striking in the handful of photographs published of them together that they stand significantly apart. None show Chaplin with an arm clutched around her shoulders, or the two of them in a mother-and-son embrace. They stand smiling for the camera like strangers who have just been introduced.

And then, out of the Far East in 1922, up popped Wheeler Dryden to see the woman who was his mother, too. Hannah, who hadn't seen her third son since he was six months old, pretended to recognize him and invited him to stay for a cup of tea.

Why both Charlie and Sydney had long given their half-brother the brush-off, ignoring his letters, can only be guessed at. But if they had regarded him as a threat to their close fraternal pairing, that passed. Sydney became fond of his kid brother with a flare for the dramatic, and Charlie would give Wheeler a job at the studio.

The family saga came to an abrupt end toward the last days of the 1928 summer. Hannah fell ill with an infection and was moved to a hospital in Burbank, a Los Angeles suburb. She was enduring agonies, and now Chaplin visited her daily, making the effort to distract her, joking about the old days.

Charlie was at the studio when the message came that she had died moments before. He rushed out and endured a last hour with the body of the woman who had passed on her gift for mimicry. He shed tears that had been accumulating since the London Bow bells first sounded in his ears.

Hannah, who had early dreamed of joining the company of theater greats, was buried in Hollywood Forever Cemetery, within sight of the graves of such luminous film celebrities as Rudolph Valentino and, soon to arrive, Douglas Fairbanks. It was as if Charlie had arranged for her to have names to drop in heaven.

CHAPTER TWENTY-SEVEN

THE IMPERTINENT GESTURE

CHAPLIN WOULD OFTEN GATHER A FEW FRIENDS and take in the boxing matches on Friday nights. He had been looking for an actress to play the leading lady in *City Lights*—and there she sat at ringside.

Twenty-year-old Virginia Cherrill, a Chicago girl out of the society pages, had had no acting experience. But she possessed the young Edna Purviance look he'd been seeking. He invited her to take a screen test.

Chaplin spent patient days and filled a can of film trying to screen-test her to offer a flower and deliver a line of dialogue (in a silent film!) just as he wanted. It was perfectionism run amok. He famously photographed her flower bit in excess of one hundred takes. She began to dislike him. He began to dislike her. Convinced

The blind girl in *City Lights* (1931) offers a flower to the Little Tramp, a scene that Chaplin shot more than 100 times in pursuit of a perfect retake known only to him. The smile between director and actress was only for the camera.

he could mold her into an actress, he nevertheless kept her in the role.

The story, what fragments existed of it, went before the cameras a couple of days after Christmas, 1928. He revealed to a friend, "Everything I do is a dance." It was commonplace for him to have a drumbeat to establish a rhythm for the actors, or even a small orchestra offstage.

His plot was simple and has now become hackneyed. The hero, with empty pockets, falls in love with a girl who needs an eye operation to see again.

All Charlie had to do was fill in the blanks. The result was a patchwork of scenes that touch the deepest emotions. Slapstick and tragedy dance a minuet for a brilliant eighty-seven minutes. Here was pathos orchestrated by genius.

To earn money for the surgery, Charlie enters the boxing ring in a lopsided match against a glowering heavyweight. This is easily the funniest, most poetic fisticuffery ever filmed. Charlie loses the winner-take-all purse. He finds a job as a street sweeper, only to discover himself following an elephant. But when the flower girl, her eyesight restored, recognizes the Little Tramp as her benefactor from the sudden touch of his hand, theaters go flood-deep in tears.

It's in this film that Chaplin reveals his new skill in managing the internal juggling act of the novel length. He's matured from the one-joke comedies of his early years. His sequences now have the intricacy of an Oriental carpet.

He catches us napping when his leading man saves the life of an alcoholic millionaire, who, when drunk, showers gratitude and friendship on the Tramp. Shouldn't this extraneous farce have been shaken to the cutting-room floor? Ah, but hang on. When sober, the moneybags doesn't know Charlie from a stray dog. That's the setup. What's Charlie going to do with it?

On a tipsy night when the millionaire gives the Tramp a thousand dollars for the blind girl's operation, burglars are discovered in the house.

Now Chaplin reveals his finesse. Police are alerted and discover the thousand-dollar bankroll in the Tramp's pocket. But why worry? Charlie has an airtight alibi, doesn't he? There stands the millionaire benefactor to back him up.

Alas, no. In a scuffle, Charlie's new pal has taken a hit on the head, sobering him up. No longer recognizing Charlie, the millionaire heatedly denies giving the money to the stranger with the funny mustache. The payoff? The innocent Little Tramp is hauled off to jail.

Chaplin's working method, to endlessly shoot and reshoot in molding his scenes, was wasteful of film but not of a creator's logic. He explained to the French artist and filmmaker Jean Cocteau that "A film is like a tree: You shook it, and all that was loose and unnecessary fell away, leaving only the essential form."

City Lights had been a work in progress for three years. It premiered in January of 1931, when the public had gone sound crazy. They were watching such talkies as *All Quiet on the Western Front*, the Marx Brothers' *Animal Crackers*, and an abundance of musicals, from *The Vagabond King* to Eddie Cantor's Broadway hit *Whoopee!*

Charlie's concession to the scorned musical occurs when the Tramp swallows a pennywhistle. He hiccups an aria.

How easy it is to imagine Chaplin with his thumb at his nose, fingers fluttering in contempt at the onrushing and jabbering new films. In fact, there is such a scene as his silent film opens and the Tramp rises from a nap in the arms of a public statue. A marble hand is chiseled with fingers wide open. For a moment, the Tramp, in profile, touches his defiant nose to the marble thumb. He could count on the crowned heads of Hollywood to turn out for the preview. They would get his inside joke. He didn't need talkies to express his contempt.

But by the time of the preview, Chaplin was losing confidence in his isolated and bullheaded judgment. Disaster holding aloft a mallet, as in one of his slapsticks, might be waiting for him in the theater. Silent films had become as out-of-date as the once-stylish spats he still wore over his shoes.

Fate gave him a temporary pass. Crowds approaching the theater were so great that traffic froze. Store windows were broken by the crush of theater patrons.

City Lights was a smash hit. It made theatrical history. For its time, it sold more tickets than any talking picture ever made.

"It is a mistake to dally long in the public's adulation," he would write. "Like a soufflé, if left standing, it bogs down."

He had a train reservation to flee town the next day. A trip to Europe would give him a chance to recharge. He shut down the studio and skipped out of Hollywood for the next sixteen months.

Chapter Twenty-Eight
FIVE FRANCS A GLANCE

CHAPLIN'S TRIP TO EUROPE WAS LARGELY A headhunting trip—Charlie's head. He was invited everywhere. He had lunch with the famous Irish wit and playwright George Bernard Shaw. He spent a weekend at the estate of Winston Churchill, soon to become the British wartime prime minister. He met the soul of the emerging new India, Mahatma Gandhi, who was then in London. And there were the usual petty royals, including an obscure queen or two, and the Prince of Wales. "The world was an entertainment," he wrote in his autobiography.

But the celebrities were booted offstage when Charlie returned to his ragged past. He slipped away to see the charity school, Hanwell, where he and Sydney had somehow survived as "booby hatch" kids. On his return to England a decade before, he had discovered that the memories of abandonment and loneliness were still too fresh to be revisited.

Now he walked into the dining hall unannounced. Not much had changed. Even the smell was the same. There sat some four hundred charity boys and girls. They recognized him in a flash and were stunned. Screams and cheers went up that could be heard across the Thames River.

Chaplin entertained them with his Little Tramp walk and mishaps with his cane and the finger sleight of shooting the hat up from his head. The kids went wild. Imagine, one of them grown up to be Charlie Chaplin himself!

For the prodigal, it was coming home. He felt like "the dead returning to earth . . . I was almost physically sick with emotion."

Sydney, too, had traveled a long way since the sound of London's Bow bells had rung over the neighborhood. He was now wealthy enough to retire with his wife to the French Riviera. The two Chaplins hadn't seen each other in six years.

Charlie was mistaken in thinking that he could easily slip down to the Mediterranean for a reunion. The French, then as now, adored little Charlot, and the crowds were endless, immense, and demanding.

At his hotel in Nice, he was furious when the management imposed a five-franc admission charge to the dining room while the Tramp was having dinner. "I can't understand all this stuff," he had written years before in indelible ink. "I'm just a little nickel comedian trying to make people laugh."

If Chaplin arrived in Europe feeling as gutted as a herring, he returned to the U.S. refilled with story ideas. There had been his audience with the tall King of Belgium, who had provided a very short chair for his visitor to sit in. The elevations made clear who was the more important monarch. The real-life incident was reborn a decade later in Chaplin's *The Great Dictator*—one of his most farcical scenes.

Always on his mind was the financial depression that was spreading around the world, following the great crash of 1929. He couldn't escape its cruelties. He had long read books on economic theory and now engaged in conversations with the wealthy upper crust of Europe. Some, like Lady Astor and her set in England, were early Fascists about to disgrace themselves by giving their support to the mad German dictator Adolf Hitler as he spawned World War II.

Chaplin expressed his workhouse sentiments to bemused ears.

He became a political rebel, throwing in his lot with the short-changed and the underprivileged. Like many other intellectuals of the 1930s, he was mesmerized by the Russian experiment in communism. But his curiosity and commitment went only so far. He never chose to join anything but the human race.

He had long before detected greed as the force driving modern times. Factories, with their speed-ups to fatten profits, he scorned as dehumanizing.

Voilà! There was the title for his next picture—*Modern Times!*

All he needed to do was find the story and a new leading lady. If he had learned nothing else from *City Lights*, it was never again to cast a society woman. Virginia Cherrill had actually asked for time off from shooting so she could have her hair done.

An unspoken hope on the European trip had been that he might find an enduring romance to balance his life. The heartthrobs were there, but he had to wait until he returned to California to find his elusive love story.

Modern Times was the first of Chaplin's films to boast an actual script. Long before, he had cast a small, vivacious Broadway actress as a carefree street gamine in a role taking shape on paper. Her name was Paulette Goddard.

Paulette Goddard, who played the barefoot leading lady in Chaplin's *Modern Times* (1936), also married the comedian. They lived happily ever after—for the next six years.

She was a free-spirited platinum blonde in her twenties, once divorced. He had persuaded her to become a brunette for the part. As Charlie's new, barefooted leading lady, she danced and twirled with the abandon of a gypsy all the way to stardom.

As an actress, she worked well with Chaplin. He'd have to have been blind not to fall in love with her. And fall he did.

In the famous fade-out scene that ends the film, she and Chaplin hold hands and walk down a country road to an unknown but smiling future. In real life, they took a slow boat to China.

And got married.

As for *Modern Times*, Charlie turned the film loose on a world in depression in 1936. It would have to fend for itself.

In addition to its power as the closing curtain to *Modern Times*, this shot of Chaplin and Goddard walking toward an unknown future proved to be the Little Tramp's final moment in the movies. With the arrival of the talkies, Chaplin felt he had no other choice but to say good-bye to his iconic but silent creation.

CHAPTER TWENTY-NINE
THE RED FLAG

WATCHING THE FIRST TEN MINUTES OR SO OF *Modern Times* could be perilous. You could die laughing. The scenes are that funny.

Charlie's on a factory production line when the conveyor belt speeds up to increase products and profits. With a wrench in each hand, the Little Tramp must tighten bolts so fast that his hands never stop. Falling behind, he is drawn into the monster machine and is spun through gears and cog wheels until he's spit out like a watermelon seed.

An eating contraption is tested to feed workers at the production lines, thus avoiding time lost for lunch periods. Charlie is chosen as reluctant guinea pig. Naturally, the mad invention smokes, sparks, and misbehaves. Feeding the victim a revolving ear of corn, the

Charlie, as a factory worker, is drawn into the machinery in *Modern Times* (1936). The movie warns, with broad laughter, of the inhumanity lurking in a society of nuts and bolts with greed as the lubricant.

machine accelerates. Spinning with the speed of a top, the ear passes before Charlie's teeth like a harmonica.

Again, in a brilliant salute to classic farce, in the mode of the banana skin on the circus high wire, he rigged the machine to throw a Mack Sennett pie at his face.

The remainder of the film is merely funny. It's the first film in which the gentle, love-smitten Little Tramp wins the girl at the end. And Chaplin makes entertainment history when he performs a novelty cabaret ditty—and sings aloud.

The public had never heard Charlie's voice before and flocked to the theater. The voice was agreeable. The trouble was that you couldn't understand a word of the song. It was delivered in gibberish, an improvised medley of languages, largely mock Italian and French.

This was not so much a concession to the bullying presence of talkies as another expression of contempt. Once again, he had decided to buck the tide of sound with a full-length pantomime. But this time, he added a background musical score.

He wrote it himself.

Defying reason, a fable has grown up that this was fakery, that he couldn't read a note. One wonders how, in his early days in vaudeville, he could have managed violin tutoring and hours of practice without some music literacy. Once famous, he performed as a guest orchestra conductor. One can hardly get away with conducting by ear.

His critics, soon to grow blustery and noisy, overlooked his meager but tuneful inheritance. His father had written songs, a couple of them successful. Charlie exhibited a rich gift for melody. He was not equipped to notate or orchestrate his scores, however, and for this he hired gifted collaborators.

Taking his cue from the operas of Richard Wagner, he bestowed a musical theme on each of the leading characters in *Modern Times*. His haunting melody for the Tramp and the gamine falling in love became a popular song—and more. It has become a standard. It is called "Smile."

An early sequence in the film makes one sit up. Not so much for its comedy, but for its bull's-eye prophecy. Had he failed as a comedian, he might have excelled at reading tea leaves.

A red flag warning of a long load falls off a lumber truck. Charlie picks up the flag and hurries after the truck to return it. A throng of revolutionaries turns a corner and marches behind Charlie as he waves the red flag—the feared color of the Russian Bolsheviks.

The police take Charlie to be the mob's rabble-rousing leader, and he is arrested.

Life was to imitate art—Charlie's, at least. In interviews he had been forthright in his unpopular views on social change, favoring the wretched and the powerless. He was accused of waving the red flag of communism. Later, a man of calm reserve, he would explain, "I am not a communist agitator. I am an agitator for peace." His denials did little good. The Federal Bureau of Investigation began making notes on him.

Modern Times inherited Chaplin's gift for survival. It gave a shrug to political witch-hunting and is regarded as one of the great and memorable American classic comedies.

CHAPTER THIRTY

WELCOME TO TOMANIA

THE LITTLE TRAMP HAD TO DIE.

Chaplin would have to abandon the fight against upstart sound or be dismissed as old-fashioned. What options remained? Making a talking film? Giving the Tramp quirky dialogue to speak?

"This was unthinkable," Chaplin wrote. "The first word he ever uttered would transform him into another person." The irrepressible Little Tramp would have to have made his last curtain call.

Who could possibly replace him in Chaplin's repertory company?

By a curious act of fate, the antic Chaplin and the satanic German dictator Adolf Hitler were born within four days of each other. Each affected the same absurd stub of a black mustache.

The contemporaries would never meet, except across the battlefield of the arts. Hitler's German armies were spreading

Europe like the Black Death. The Second World War was about to break out.

Among the dictator's historic lunacies was the plan to murder every Jewish man, woman, and child in Europe. The slaughter had begun.

Chaplin reacted in fury. When he pasted on his mustache, as if about to sniff up a domino, he took on an uncanny resemblance to the German mass murderer. Why not play Hitler in his next film? He'd make it a killer satire. Once again, he'd risk marrying farce to tragedy.

But where would he find the farce? Recalling his boyhood job as a lather boy in a barbershop next to a graveyard, he saw the opportunity in playing dual roles as a little Jewish barber who is a dead ringer for the bloody dictator.

Late in 1938, Chaplin began his usual process of reaching into the cosmos to grope for scenes in hiding. Like many authors, he was not in the habit of figuring out his endings in advance; he left them to chance. But this was to be a sound film with a detailed script. He'd give the ending some thought.

Meanwhile, Paulette was at home in the all-but-empty, brooding yellow house on the hill. She cheered things up by painting a couple of rooms pink, to Charlie's snorts. She put fresh flowers everywhere except his bedroom, for he labored under the notion that flowers absorbed oxygen. He did not intend to share his slumbers with botanical house guests.

Before long, Chaplin's two young sons, Sydney, age five, and Charles Jr., seven, had sleepover privileges in their father's mansion. They could be expected to love the private swimming pool, the movie projection room, the gold faucets, the pipe organ, the tennis court—but especially did they love Paulette Goddard.

"Syd and I lost our hearts to Paulette at once," Charles Jr. would write. She was playful and adoring; she was sunlight. When very young, they were allowed to sleep in her bed.

Charlie was at his best when he was working. He was also at his worst. He was too focused to spare more than perfunctory hellos for his sons and little more for Paulette.

The marriage began to falter, but *The Great Dictator* was emerging from its creator's sweet-and-sour imagination. At the end of a year, he had a shooting script of immense length—some three hundred pages. The usual script was a hundred or so.

Chaplin was a genius only when he was working. At liberty, he bought a boat but rarely stepped aboard. He was not notably social but endured social events as a shy presence, unless asked to do his funny Little Tramp walk or otherwise perform. Out of the flare of a spotlight, who was he?

Chaplin had had his studio refitted for sound. He began to shoot *The Great Dictator*, his first talkie, in September 1939, a week after Hitler invaded Poland to ignite World War II.

Chaplin chose to aim his story at the deadly nightmare facing the Jews in paranoid Germany. In the film, the country is given the poisonous name Tomania. He cast Paulette in the role of Hannah, a Jewish ghetto orphan. Hannah? Wasn't that the name of his mother?

It was predictable that the gentle look-alike barber would be mistaken for the screaming look-alike dictator, here called Adenoid Hynkel. Chaplin had much more up his sleeve. He would skewer the pompous Italian dictator Mussolini as well.

And there's the comic scene inspired by the king of Belgium. The movie's two tyrants, in barber chairs, continue to ratchet themselves higher and higher in a battle of egos.

Charlie, as an insignificant Jewish barber, is mistaken for a fictional dictator, largely as a parody of the monster of World War II, whose mustache was Chaplinesque. Here, the dictator does a ballet with a balloon representing the world he intends to capture.

This is quickly followed by the greatest ballet since Tchaikovsky's *Swan Lake*. Hitler/Hynkel choreographs a rhapsodic dance with a huge balloon of the world, soon to be his prize of war. It bursts in his face.

Again, the wizard's brew of the sinister and the slapstick worked. The film was a box-office sellout everywhere but in Germany, with its goose-stepping new breed of Huns.

CHAPTER THIRTY-ONE
THE PHANTOM JEW

ON THE ASSUMPTION THAT CHAPLIN WAS JEWISH, Hitler banned him from Germany. A piece of propaganda sneered, "This little Jewish tumbler, as disgusting as he is boring."

The gossip that Chaplin was among the chosen people attached itself to him like a hidden birthmark. But it was the other brother, it was Sydney whose father was Jewish, right? Not Charlie?

Nevertheless, when it moved him, Charlie forthrightly claimed to be part Jewish. Or when it moved him—not.

Returning from Europe in 1922, he met a very bright dark-haired child on the ship, and this conversation followed.

"You must be Spanish," I tell her.

"Oh no, not Spanish; I'm Jewish," she answers.

"That accounts for your genius."

"Oh, do you think Jewish people are clever?" she asks, eagerly.

"Of course. All great geniuses had Jewish blood in them. No, I'm not Jewish," as she is about to put the question, "but I'm sure there must be some somewhere in me. I hope so."

No, yes, perhaps. After all, he did regard himself as something of a genius, and being Jewish might help.

Here he is in 1924, in a meeting with production executives planning a big-budget life of Christ. Charlie wanted the lead. "I'm the logical choice. I look the part, I'm a Jew, and I'm a comedian." Did he envision himself doing shtick while walking on water? He didn't get the part.

Chaplin's biographers have been in a guessing game over Chaplin's mysterious bloodline. Was he a descendant, through his father, of French Jews? The source for this bit of fantasy may have been young Chaplin himself, embracing Fontainebleau as his birthplace, giving himself airs, and staking out the possibility of a Gallic-Jewish connection.

Later, when Chaplin was thirty-six years old, he made news by attributing his shortness, his dark curly hair, and Mediterranean skin, as gifts from a part-Spanish Gypsy grandmother on his mother's side. Hannah, he said, had just told him so.

Another bedazzlement to shoot down the old gossip? Did it work? Not much.

Could Hannah be believed? Could Chaplin?

The suspicion persisted.

Regarding Hannah, he was to recall that when relatively young "he had lost faith in the romantic stories she had told him about her . . . and in her claim that the drunken entertainer for whom he was named was really his father."

Who, then, could his father have been if not Hannah's boozy husband?

In the two months that he and Sydney lived under their father's roof as children, Charlie would gaze at Charles senior and wonder how he could be related to this man, with his oxen bones. They didn't seem to match Charlie's own bird-thin skeleton. And why didn't he possess the man's strong, self-assured profile, as Sydney did?

It was more than a child could fathom.

An adult at last, Chaplin was warm and genial when he was moved to deny a Jewish progenitor. He might graciously state,

"I don't have that honor." And then he'd contradict himself in the next magazine interview, declaring that he *was* "of Jewish extraction." And then contradict himself again by explaining that he chose not to make denials, as that would only cheer the anti-Semites among us. In sum, he appeared to change his answer as often as his spats.

It's clear that Chaplin himself cannot be regarded as a reliable witness any more than a chameleon can attest to its own color.

To unravel the Jewish mystery within a Christian enigma, it's first necessary to riddle out Sydney. One can assume from photographs that Sydney's father was not a Jewish gambler named Sidney Hawkes, with a banished vowel in the first name. Sydney was growing up as something of a mirror image of his stepfather, Charles Chaplin senior. Even the family noticed.

And if Hannah doubted that the boozy senior Charles was young Charlie's real father—who was? Most likely someone very short and handsome with curly hair and Mediterranean coloring. Someone more like the Little Tramp.

The only other gent attached to the early Hannah chronicle is that mysterious charmer and London Jew, Sidney Hawkes.

Hannah was not known to be a faithful wife. In his autobiography,

Charles Chaplin

The riddle of Charlie Chaplin's ancestry is hard to solve. As these photos show, his half-brother Sydney (at right) bore a striking resemblance to the man the family called Sydney's stepfather—Charles Chaplin, Sr. (on the left). How does the London Jew and roving gambling man Sidney Hawkes fit into the family tree if he was not, after all, Sydney's father? Was he Charlie's?

Charles applies thick makeup to his mother's past character by stating up front, "To gauge the morals of our family by commonplace standards would be as erroneous as putting a thermometer in boiling water." At least two of Hannah's children were illegitimate; possibly all three.

Even she was uncertain who Charlie's father really was.

With Hawkes, the trail of suspects for fatherhood stops cold. No photographs of the mysterious suitor have survived. His name has turned to dust.

In his lifetime, if the technology had existed, Chaplin might have undergone a DNA search to clear up the clinging mystery of his life. Today, as revealed in the final chapter of this book, it would be necessary to jackhammer through tons of cement to get at Chaplin's coffin and extract a sample for testing—or one might be obtained more simply from one of his children. But all the procedure might determine is whether the senior Charles was Charlie's father. Where would one find a test sample from the phantom Sidney Hawkes?

CHAPTER THIRTY-TWO

THE COCKNEY CAD

CHARLIE'S FALL FROM PUBLIC GRACE WAS SUDDEN and steep and just around the corner.

The Great Dictator was an immense hit, except in Germany, where a print was smuggled in for Hitler to screen. His reaction has not been recorded. One can only imagine that had Charlie remained in England, Hitler would have hastened his invasion to get his hands on the insolent little Cockney.

Some critics felt it was irreverent to mix the fantasies of slapstick with the realities of so cruel a war. The atrocities of the Holocaust had not yet emerged; Chaplin confessed that had he known of the unique barbarities hidden in Germany, he would have found it impossible to make the film.

But it was early in the war, and most critics agreed with the

New York Herald Tribune in August 1940, when it judged the film, "a savage comic commentary on a world gone mad."

With regrets, Chaplin and Paulette Goddard divorced in Mexico in 1942. Freed from his controlling persona, she went on to a broadly successful film career. She eventually married a famous novelist and moved to Europe.

Two new women entered his life. The first was as toxic as Typhoid Mary, whose eager touch passed along her dreaded disease. The girl was a disturbed, aspiring, reckless, redheaded actress named Joan Barry.

Charlie footed the bill for her acting lessons and got on with preparing a new film about Bluebeard, the notorious wife murderer.

If little time had been needed for Charlie to fall into a passing romance, it took four years to clear out the wreckage. One night Chaplin returned to his yellow house on the hill and discovered that the spurned redhead had broken a window to gain entry. And she had a pistol in her hand.

He softly talked her into a calmer state. A week later, she was back, and he called the police.

In the midst of the tawdry drama, he met the profound and

enduring love of his life. She was Oona O'Neill, the daughter of the great American playwright Eugene O'Neill.

They met at a small dinner party. Oona—a New York debutante, tall, with straight black hair—had abandoned Vassar College to explore an ambition to become an actress.

Charlie, then in his early fifties, offered to guide her in her career. Instead in June 1943, he and Oona were married. It created something of a scandal. She was eighteen, and her father, the playwright, was so furious he disowned her. She never saw him again in her lifetime. She wrote him from time to time, never receiving a reply.

She worshipped Chaplin. His devotion to her was unmatched in his other marriages. The newlyweds survived public hissing with indifference and celebrated one of the most successful and enduring marriages in Hollywood.

But Joan Barry was far from finished with the comedian. She had had a daughter and swore that he was the father. She hired a lawyer and brought a paternity suit.

Entire forests of newspaper pulp were consigned to the newest Hollywood scandal.

Oona O'Neill and Charlie in their first public appearance after their marriage in 1943. Theirs became one of the showcase and enduring Hollywood marriages. They would have eight children.

"A Cockney cad!" the emotional prosecuting attorney shouted at the top of his lungs. And after three decades in the United States, why hadn't the English swine become one of us—a citizen? And everyone knew he was a pinko. A bloody communist, no doubt!

Chaplin was convicted. But not on the evidence.

He might be guilty of loyalty to his native country, of irritating and unpopular political views, but not of fathering Joan Barry's beautiful baby. Blood tests revealed Miss Barry to be type A. Her baby, type B. Charlie was type O. It was impossible for him to be the father.

The testimony was stoutly ignored as scientific voodoo by the court. Chaplin was directed to support the little girl until she reached the age of twenty-one. He did.

Miss Barry slowly, slowly vanished from sight. She was found wandering the streets and eventually sheltered in the state mental hospital, where she completely passed from Chaplin's life.

He had been unable to work under the persistent distractions and public abuse that was slung at him so righteously. Seven years would go down the drain before he made another film, *Monsieur Verdoux*. The tale of a natty, real-life Frenchman with a nasty habit of poisoning his many wives was largely murdered at the box office.

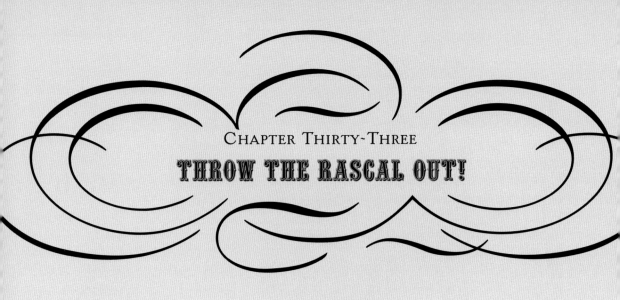

Chapter Thirty-Three
THROW THE RASCAL OUT!

UNABLE TO ALLOW THE LITTLE TRAMP TO RISE from the ashes with an implausible film voice, Chaplin had had to find other skins to inhabit. Once again, he would mix styles by portraying a killer in what he termed "A Comedy of Murders" boldly above the title: *Monsieur Verdoux*.

Chaplin trimmed himself a narrow mustache as sharp as an ice pick and embarked on a tale of mayhem for profit. After raiding his victims' funds, Verdoux disposes of his wives' corpses in his backyard incinerator. Neighbors notice the black smoke frequently billowing out, but their suspicions are untouched.

Given the revelation that the Germans had efficiently disposed of six million Jews in immense, smoking gas ovens, Chaplin's choice of backyard ovens might seem reckless and insensitive to the extreme.

Chaplin transformed himself again in 1946—from a tramp to a dapper murderer—with a change of hats and a mustache pointed enough for sewing needles. His screenplay for *Monsieur Verdoux* won an Academy Award nomination the next year, but the picture was murdered in the theaters.

That would be a misreading. The incinerator vividly served Chaplin's theme. He designed his raspy comedy to dramatize the seduction of human kindness and civilized behavior by business avarice, personal greed, and hard times. Monsieur Verdoux didn't have to be a German Nazi to become a barbarian. He was a common bourgeois in an immaculate waistcoat and starched winged collar, converted to barbarism by circumstances. He was a middle-class nobody with a backyard oven of his own.

In this, Chaplin anticipated by almost twenty years the writer Hannah Arendt's famous summing-up of the insolent Nazi mind as "the banality of evil."

The critics approached this film as warily as poison ivy. There were funny scenes, especially the ones with the exuberant comic actress Martha Raye. But the general opinion held that this film was minor Chaplin.

Charlie was infuriated with the hostility of the once-cheering Americans. Despite the hostility, though, the screenplay was nominated in 1947 for an Academy Award.

At this stage in his career, fame had matured some of his moodiest traits. He was showing little concern for the feelings of others. He cruelly turned his back on such loyal old friends as Edna Purviance and Henry Bergman, a portly supporting player who dated back to Charlie's silent days. On the set he treated his younger half-brother—Wheeler Dryden, serving as assistant director—with loud abuse.

If he had begun his professional life by holding a mirror to the human comedy, he was now mesmerized by his own dazzling reflection. He was apt to skip close-ups of supporting actors, declaiming, "People come to see me."

His fellow comedian and vaudeville roommate Stan Laurel had detected a duality in Chaplin's behavior in their earliest days. He had found Charlie off-stage to be a wallflower-shy member of the troupe who turned bold and harum-scarum before an audience or the camera. Now world-famous, Chaplin could be genial, kind, and generous while harboring an offscreen Mr. Hyde.

He could be imperious in his kingdom, verbally whiplashing his actors on the set. No one was safe from his tinderbox flare-ups.

Naturally he collected resentful assistants who regarded him as a monster and waited for him to take a fall.

He came close to accommodating them when the communist scare of the late 1940s embroiled him. A committee of congressmen in Washington went on what has come to be called a witch hunt for

Stan Laurel, who became half of the famous comedy team Laurel and Hardy, came over on the boat from England with Chaplin. In their early vaudeville days together, Laurel detected a duality in Chaplin's nature. He could be genial and kind but then could turn on his actors and film crews.

communists, their sympathizers, and spies lurking in the shadows.

Called the House Un-American Activities Committee, the politicians galloped around the land making themselves famous and infamous. They discovered that the biggest headlines could be created about the movie folks. The committee promptly descended on Hollywood. They fancied themselves remounted Paul Reveres on whitewashed horses, riding to the nation's rescue. They unleashed seven years of hoopla for themselves and vilification for their victims.

Chaplin looked like a pushover. Through the years he had been observed as a noisy political rebel with a red Russian paintbrush in hand. The committee called him to the witness stand. "Proceed with the butchery," said Chaplin in his opening remarks.

In the past, his great fame had barricaded him from such gadflies as these blustering politicians from Washington. But now they seemed content to ride roughshod over the First Amendment to the U.S. Constitution, which guarantees its citizens free speech and thought. Their trump card was to charge uncooperative witnesses with contempt of Congress.

The inquisitor, to Charlie, "Are you a Communist?"

"I am not a Communist!" came Charlie's forthright answer.

Was he a sympathizer? Yes, he supposed he was. Like so many other world figures, he had been in favor of opening a second front during World War II to distract the Germans in the Nazi invasion of our ally at the time, Russia. The truth was, he had always been a bit starry-eyed about Russia's new form of government, favoring the working class and the underdog. He seemed able to give Russian dictatorship, which he later abhorred, a temporary pass.

The committee sent ten film writers to jail for refusing to answer its questions. Chaplin confounded the committee by answering fully but providing nothing felonious. His wrists unfettered, Chaplin freely walked out of the ballroom of the Hotel Gotham in New York, where the hearing was being held. Today, the episodes are generally bracketed with the witchcraft persecutions in Salem, Massachusetts, two hundred and fifty years before.

But Washington wasn't through with this upstart Cockney. The FBI continued its gaze into his activities. J. Edgar Hoover, head of the sleuths, hunted for someone to denounce Chaplin as a secret communist. It was 1952, and still no luck.

Meanwhile, some women's groups were tireless in their bombast aimed at his marriages to women so much younger than he was. As for his loyalty to America, the cry was gaining volume: Why, after thirty years' residence and money-getting in Hollywood, had he never applied for citizenship?

He felt cut. Many Americans thriving in England had clung to their U.S. citizenship. Many in Hollywood's English colony remained citizens of their home country. Why was he obliged to turn his back on the island of his birth? Money? The bulk of his pictures' earnings came from abroad, and he paid U.S. taxes on them.

But the din grew ever noisier.

Foreigner! Deport him! Throw the rascal out!

CHAPTER THIRTY-FOUR
SO LONG, CHARLIE

CREATIVE ARTISTS COMMONLY SACK THEIR PASTS like vandals. Charlie did it in a film about his early years in English vaudeville. Like *The Kid* of decades earlier, his 1952 feature, *Limelight*, was an adventure in film autobiography.

Despite the public demand for tar and feathers, Chaplin had preoccupied himself with writing out at great length the dual story he envisioned for dramatizing the rise and fall of a famous comedian.

He cast a dark-haired English star, Claire Bloom, as a ballerina whose legs have become paralyzed. How like his mother, whose singing voice and career were taken by sudden paralysis.

Chaplin, as Calvero, the great clown, has experienced the theft of his own career by age. He no longer seems able to make an audience laugh.

He gets the ballerina back on her dancing legs. A May-December romance develops. Chaplin spends the next two hours pulling strings for a bittersweet ending.

The Chaplins now had four kids, and Charlie used all of them in the movie, including his oldest daughter, Geraldine. She grew up to become a successful film actress and would play her own grandmother, Hannah, in a 1992 movie biography of her father.

Limelight was the last film Chaplin would shoot at his own studio. On his way to London with his family aboard the *Queen Elizabeth*, he was notified by cable that his U.S. reentry permit had been lifted. He was not welcome back. The Attorney General was throwing him out.

Out, and branded as an undesirable alien.

Charlie was furious! He was insulted! "This was not the day of great artists," he said bitterly in London, in that crepe-hung year of 1952. "It was the day of politics." Immediately he sent Oona back to Hollywood to close up their affairs, sell his studio and the yellow house on the hill. He was convinced that he would never again place his famous feet on U.S. soil. Nor would he forgive his assassins.

These were not custard pies being thrown at him now. They were the orange peels and rotten tomatoes he had dodged in his youth.

The last film he would make in his own studio was *Limelight*, a tender story set in the vaudeville days of his past. He was barred from returning to the United States after a trip to Europe and passed through these famous gates for the last time in 1952.

Charlie and Oona arrive in France. While America slammed its door to him, the French were soon to bestow its Legion of Honor award on Chaplin.

His footprints in cement in the forecourt of Grauman's Chinese Theatre were regarded as box-office poison and jackhammered into rubble. Movie columnists, such as the queen of them all, ultraconservative Hedda Hopper, roasted him on spits almost daily. The American Legion, not waiting for the FBI to come up with evidence of traitorous dabblings, got an armlock on theater owners to ban Chaplin films. They succeeded.

It was the same year of his deportation, 1952, that the French government awarded him its Legion of Honor.

Like refugees, the Chaplins roamed about Europe in five-star hotels. After a few months, Charlie bought a country house on thirty-seven parklike acres in Corsier-sur-Vevey, Switzerland. The house had fifteen rooms. To fill the added space, Charlie and Oona would have four more kids, for a total of eight.

Twenty years needed to pass before the fears and noisemakers of the 1950s became a public embarrassment and *Limelight* was seen at last by American audiences.

In 1972, it received five Academy Award nominations. Chaplin had composed a haunting background melody that became a hit song.

Charlie, the great artist, had outlived his assassins.

Oona standing on the grounds of the Swiss country estate, Manor de Ban, that became home for the rest of Charlie's life.

CHAPTER THIRTY-FIVE

TAKES AND MISTAKES

UNLIKE NAPOLEON'S LONELY EXILE TO ELBA WITH a view of the chilly Atlantic, Chaplin on his large estate enjoyed the comforts of a dozen servants and a view of Lake Geneva. The cosmic absurdity of a poorhouse kid living in such splendor was not lost on him. Still, he had met kings and queens and princes, none of whom were his equals as creative artists. He was entitled to his theatrical purple.

It would seem that he was now problem-proof except for the conundrum of how a country gentleman in his mid-sixties, his hair Alpine white, should confront his inexhaustible energies. He would make another comedy, of course.

He unknowingly embarked on a great novelty. Charlie Chaplin

went to a vast amount of trouble to make a first for him—a very bad film.

No one brings forth a misbegotten movie on purpose. *A King in New York* was Charlie on a very bad day. His films were truly handcrafted. He wrote them, produced and directed them, acted in them, edited them, and wrote the music. Alas, he could share the blame only with himself. But wasn't he allowed one potboiler in a long career of original and idiosyncratic work?

The footage is not without its brilliant Chaplinesques. The exiled king of the title, after face surgery, sits with frozen expression as he watches comics perform while trying not to laugh and burst his stitches. In a deafening restaurant he resorts to mimicry to order caviar, from catching and gutting the sturgeon to spreading the eggs on toast. And turtle soup, with a plate like a shell over one hand. Easy for him.

The plot is not so tasty and seems to have been conceived in a fit of pique. Costumed in the garb of satire, the dead-broke king of New York becomes embroiled with a hostile government and eventually flees the country and its modern grotesqueries.

Evidently, Charlie had forgotten his early contempt for the

Shakespearean stories of lofty kings and queens. But if he stepped into his own trap, it wasn't because his rendering of a deposed monarch lacked humanity and conviction. It was the wit. It was the gags. Both were starved for oxygen.

As in the film, Chaplin had severed his ties to the United States. He had disposed of the studio to a real-estate firm at a bargain price of $700,000. The new owner sold off half of the five acres. What remains is now the home of the Jim Henson Company and the Muppets. A soundstage is often rented out for weddings, bar mitzvahs, and other affairs.

Charlie was a major holder of stock in United Artists, once prosperous, currently a million dollars in debt. He sold off his stake for pocket change.

The past was in pursuit. His younger half-brother, Wheeler Dryden, left behind in Hollywood, died a virtual recluse. His demise was followed a few months later by Chaplin's early leading lady, Edna Purviance. That same year, 1958, his star was excluded from Hollywood's celebrated Walk of Fame. But that was not the end of the story.

Offstage, Chaplin decided it was time to fulfill a promise to his

Kermit the Frog, dressed as the Little Tramp, now reigns over the entrance to the former Chaplin studios.

English publisher to sculpt out an autobiography, and he set to his labors.

No ghostwriter needed apply. After a morning swim, he dictated page after page to a secretary. Then, repeating his process in film-making, he treated these pages as preliminary takes. He patiently made new takes, rereading and rewriting. The memoir "will take me at least another year to finish," he wrote his actor son Charles. The result was a polished manuscript of some five hundred pages, published in 1964. The arts, as Mozart among others proved, were not for the indolent.

The book is a warm and admirable autobiography for what's in it, and in the manner of most autobiographies, a curiosity for what's left out. It's not surprising that nowhere in his text does *A King in New York* get a mention, but neither does the death of his younger half-brother. And we are left to wonder what quite happened to his older brother, Sydney, after Charlie settled in Vevey for the next quarter-century. Though a wealthy man, Sydney appears to have lived out his life frugally in a trailer home on the French Riviera. He visited his now-baronial brother, where Charlie's children regarded him as their eccentric uncle. He died in Nice, France, in 1965.

Somewhat on the pattern of cavalierly withholding close-ups of his leading players, Chaplin skips the comedians in his old film repertory company. What would *Easy Street* and other films have been without the mountainous villainies of Eric Campbell? Charlie again finds little room under the klieg lights for anyone but himself. He was completely silent on his early vaudeville coworker and rival Stan Laurel. The fellow Englishman was extremely generous through the years in his public praise of Chaplin.

But these are small curiosities. At the same time, the autobiographer made space to indulge his chief sport, after tennis, of name-dropping.

As if fixed in time by the oft-noted Dickensian poverty of his childhood, he seems forever the hungry kid peering through the window at the great folks inside.

He sees himself dining on white tablecloths with the president of France, the queen of Spain, and the former movie beauty Princess Grace of Monaco. If he goes slumming, it is with such celebrity riffraff as Pablo Picasso, Graham Greene, John Steinbeck, and Somerset Maugham. If he read the novelist William Faulkner, he may well have paused at the line, "The past isn't dead. It's not even past." He seems forever to be assuring himself that he's no longer out in the mean Kennington streets.

The autobiography, like almost every work he touched, was an immense success. It was translated into a Babel of languages. It earned the triumphant comedian a fortune that he no longer needed.

A contemporary joke sums up his essence in a few words. At a party, he sings an opera aria—magnificently, even hitting high C. An admirer says, "Bravo, Charlie! You could have been a great opera star!"

"No," the comedian answers. "I can't sing. I can only mimic."

The curtain did not fall on his own story with Charlie walking away along a lonely road to an unknowable future. He knew what lay ahead. He had another film idea crackling off the synapses in his brain. He had twenty years yet to live, some of them under the razzle-dazzle and limelights of Hollywood. He would become famous all over again.

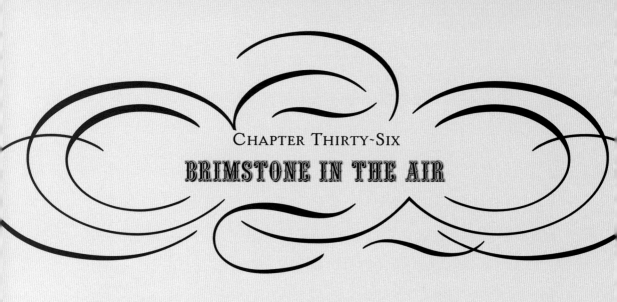

CHAPTER THIRTY-SIX
BRIMSTONE IN THE AIR

DECADES EARLIER CHAPLIN HAD PLAYED WITH an idea for a full-length comedy about a woman stowing away in a gentleman's cabin on an ocean liner in the Far East.

Now he would do it, taking the entire year of 1966 to make a bedroom farce with very little farce. He would cast the Italian mega-star Sophia Loren as the runaway woman and Marlon Brando, the famously brilliant actor, in the comedy role of the cabin passenger. What could go wrong?

Everything. Chaplin was now a cherubic seventy-seven years old and suitable to play only geriatric leading men. He had the wisdom to deal himself out of *A Countess from Hong Kong* except for a walk-on cameo as a ship's steward given to seasickness. A Chaplin film without Chaplin was champagne without the bubbles.

From his earliest film days, Charlie was infamous for showing each actor, to the smallest detail, exactly how he wanted the part played. He regarded his behavior as an artist's perfectionism. The term was not yet in use, but today he would be seen as the ultimate control freak.

On the set, a spectacle of artistic angers flared. Chaplin attempted to show Brando, the world's finest actor, how to act. Brimstone smoked up the air. Brando respected the famous clown, but he was not interested in becoming an imitation Chaplin. After a severe bawling out for being inexcusably late on the set, Brando was sufficiently chastised to find a workable truce. Years later he characterized Chaplin as "a fearsomely cruel man."

Returning rich on a trip to England, Chaplin had noted years before, "The saddest thing I can imagine is to get used to luxury." He might have issued the same warning about fame and its attendant hazards. Ego had mobilized him into a tyrannical old man. His children in the Swiss manor house were allowed to see only Charlie Chaplin films.

The public liked *A Countess from Hong Kong* more than the critics, who generally dismissed it as a disaster.

It would be his last film. He was living the tragedy of a man who had outlived his genius.

He disagreed. His old gifts had not deserted him. As a young vaudevillian he was expert at "taking the nap"—theatrical argot for "faking a slap" or blow. Probably Cockney rhyming slang.

In the matter of quitting, he took a nap. He faked a reaction. Let the critics think what they wished. He talked of writing an opera and even of bringing back the Little Tramp.

Nothing came of these airy projects.

But if any life was spring-loaded with surprises, it was his. The U.S. government was willing to embrace and make up. The decade of red-baiting for hidden communists had faded. For all its efforts, the FBI had found nothing to pin on Chaplin that it could take to court. The comedian was merely a public nuisance who counted himself a citizen of the world.

Early in 1972, he was belatedly honored with a star on the Hollywood Walk of Fame. Immigration passed him through, and off he went to accept a Special Academy Award in Hollywood.

His initial nervousness at finding himself back on hostile soil quickly dissipated when he was warmly hugged by old friends, including Claire Bloom, his leading lady in *Limelight*, and his ex-wife and still good friend Paulette Goddard. For the first time in decades, he saw Jackie Coogan, the kid from *The Kid*, now a grown man, and

Letting scornful and righteous bygones be bygones, Hollywood installed Charlie's star on its Walk of Fame in 1972.

he burst into tears. He could not bring himself to revisit his old studio, then taken over by A&M Records, but drove by when it was closed and peered through the gate. There lay his past, largely concealed under a new sign and a new coat of paint.

He tortured himself into a fear that no one would show up to see him at the Oscar show. The place was packed. There was hardly a dry eye in the house when he was so taken by emotion he could hardly speak. He managed to express a grateful thank-you and then did his trademark trick of making a derby hat spring from his head. During the course of the evening, he stood for two ovations. Applause was his native language. He nodded, lit from within.

How can an actor top such an honor? Charlie did.

CHAPTER THIRTY-SEVEN
SIR CHARLIE

ON A MARCH DAY IN 1975, CHAPLIN WAS KNIGHTED by Queen Elizabeth II. The last few years had been unkind to a man of his prodigious energies. He suffered from gout and could walk only with difficulty. His famous shuffling amble was now beyond his ability. He tired easily. This would be his last trip to London, and it might have appeared to be a funeral cortege in rehearsal.

The orchestra, the Welsh Guards, played three of Chaplin's film songs during the course of the ceremonies. Chaplin was determined to walk straight-backed and upright to the queen, but he had to abandon all hope. He needed to be wheeled to Her Majesty. Certainly he must have regretted that the queen had not been more prompt and knighted him when he was in his prime.

When the ceremony ended, the newsmen honored Chaplin's

While he was now Sir Charlie, Chaplin's characteristic signature with iconic hat, cane, and shoes remained the same.

request not to photograph him requiring so much help to get into the limousine. When he entered the party that followed, he was a new man. He was Sir Charlie.

He sat quietly and watched the festivities.

Old age threw another grenade at Chaplin. He experienced a stroke and lingered on for two more years. And then, as if to prove he was still a master of timing, he managed to die on Christmas Day 1977. He was eighty-eight.

Two days later, under a light drizzle and a random canopy of black umbrellas, Sir Charlie was interred in the small cemetery at Vevey, Switzerland.

It would not have surprised him, with his eye for tragedy disguised as slapstick, that he would have to be buried all over again soon.

Nine weeks later, his gravesite was discovered to be an empty pit in the ground. His body had been snatched. He commanded fresh headlines around the world, like an actor's final encore and bow.

CHAPTER THIRTY-EIGHT

A LIFE IN CONCRETE

TWO AMATEUR CRIMINALS, BLOCKHEADS BOTH, had conceived a scheme to get themselves barrels of money. They would dig up Charlie Chaplin's coffin, kidnap the corpse, and hold it for ransom.

And so, in a biblical rain, Gantcho Ganev, thirty-eight, a drifter and garage mechanic from Bulgaria, and Roman Wardas, twenty-four, Polish and a fellow mechanic, sloshed around with shovels in the grave. Their original plan had a note of cunning. They would rebury the coffin even deeper and cover it over with dirt. No one would think to look for the body below in the same grave.

Ganev and Wardas didn't think to choose a more collaborative night. By the time they got out the coffin, they were quicksanded in rain and mud. Like the well in "The Sorcerer's Apprentice," the

Charlie Chaplin's Body Stolen

Swiss Police Say They Lack Clues to 'Sick' Crime

VEVEY, Switzerland (UPI)—Grave robbers have stolen the remains of Charlie Chaplin, Swiss police announced today.

Police said the coffin was dug up and taken away Wednesday night or early today.

Chaplin died on Christmas Day at the age of 88. He was buried two days later in the tiny cemetery of the village of Corsier, overlooking Lake Geneva.

"During the night of March 1 to 2, the grave of Mr. Charlie Chaplin, who died on Dec. 25, 1977, was desecrated in the cemetery of Corsier-Above-Vevey," the police statement said.

"The coffin was taken away. An investigation is under way on grounds of disturbing the peace of the dead."

Today, police said that neither they nor Chaplin's family had received any telephone calls from persons claiming to be responsible.

"We have no clues at this time as to the identity of those responsible for this very sick crime," a spokesman said.

Police did not rule out the possibility of a ransom demand for return of the coffin and Chaplin's remains.

The actor's burial had been attended by the former Oona O'Neill, Chaplin's wife of 34 years, seven of their eight children, household employes, the family doctor and Alan Rothnie, the British ambassador to Switzerland.

Rothnie represented Queen Elizabeth II, who knighted Chaplin in 1975 when the actor already was confined to a wheelchair and in failing health.

"There is now just the hole in the ground," the police official said. "We can tell that the crime occurred during the night because of the freshly dug earth."

The cemetery was placed under police guard after the theft was discovered.

The Chaplins had lived at Corsier since 1952.

A millionaire many times over, Chaplin—in order to avoid death duties—had most of his possessions, including continuing large movie royalties, put in his wife's name.

Oona, who married Chaplin when she was 18 and he 54, has been writing a book on her life with the actor.

News of the bizarre body snatch spread around the world with the speed of a lightning flash.

COFFIN IN CORNFIELD

Chaplin's Remains Found; Pair Held

LAUSANNE, Switzerland (UPI)—Swiss police Wednesday recovered the remains of Charlie Chaplin and charged two political refugees from Eastern Europe with stealing his body and demanding a $600,000 ransom.

Police said they found Chaplin's coffin buried 2 feet deep in a cornfield only 15 miles from the cemetery from where it was stolen. The recovery was made after one suspect was arrested Tuesday during a stakeout of 200 public telephones in Lausanne.

Names of the two suspects were not released but police said one was an unemployed 24-year-old Pole who received political asylum in 1973, and the other was a 38-year old Bulgarian mechanic, married and the father of one child. Both were residents of Lausanne.

The Pole had telephoned the Chaplin family several times since the bizarre grave robbery March 2, police said at a news conference. At first he set a ransom of $600,000 but later scaled it down to $250,000.

The Pole and the Bulgarian also sent the family a photograph of the comedian's coffin in an open hole in the cornfield.

Police said they twice laid a trap for the two men, pretending to be ready to pay the ransom, "but there was never any intention to pay."

It had been agreed in previous calls that "final arrangements" to pay the ransom would be made Tuesday morning, police said. They detained the Pole when he went to a pay phone and dialed the Chaplins.

The phone in the Chaplin family home in Corsier, a village above Lake Geneva, had been tapped, with the family's approval, ever since the grave robbery at the Corsier cemetery. Chaplin had lived in Corsier for 25 years before his death last Christmas Day.

The Pole confessed at once, police said, but refused to reveal the identity of his accomplice. The Bulgarian was quickly found, however, by checking the Pole's acquaintances. The Bulgarian also confessed.

They were charged with attempted extortion and disturbance of the peace of the dead. Both stand to receive prison sentences of up to 7½ years, police said.

"It appears that only the two men were involved," the statement said.

Examining magistrate Jean-Daniel Tenthorey said the coffin was found buried in a cornfield outside the village of Noville, at the eastern tip of Lake Geneva and just 15 miles from Corsier.

The coffin was taken away by hearse but will not be re-buried at Corsier until legal procedures are completed, police said.

"Everyone is very happy, very relieved," a Chaplin family spokesman said. Chaplin is believed to have left his widow, Oona, at least $25 million on his death. Oona, daughter of the late playwright Eugene O'Neill, said immediately after the theft of the coffin that she would reject any ransom demand.

"Charlie would have found it ridiculous," she said at the time.

Police said they always suspected a ransom demand would eventually be made.

"It was just a question of waiting," one police official said.

The body snatchers were rapidly put out of the kidnapping business. Chaplin was reburied in concrete.

grave kept refilling as fast as the robbers could shovel it out. They improvised a new plan.

After dragging the coffin to their car, the body snatchers buried it twenty miles away (newspaper accounts said twelve), in the privacy of a cornfield.

How could they now fail to become rich when they phoned Sir Charlie's wife, Lady Chaplin? They demanded 600,000 Swiss francs, then, as now, a great fortune. It was the first of twenty-seven telephone calls they made, with brilliant stupidity, almost all from the nearby city of Lausanne.

They might as well have put in their ransom calls directly to the police. At each agreed-upon time for the criminals' next demand—surely from an anonymous telephone booth—the police stationed a cop to watch every public call box in the city.

Wardas and Ganev were nabbed and snapped in handcuffs. They were tried and convicted in mid-December 1978. Among the charges was "disturbing the peace of the dead."

Sir Charlie was respectfully reburied, his casket encased in tons of cement. His fugitive burial site in the cornfield is now marked and draws visitors from around the world.

Chaplin's estate was estimated at $90 million. It was not enough to protect Lady Chaplin from twenty years of alcoholism after Charlie's death. Given the boozy demise of Charles senior, nothing could have disturbed the star's repose more. He himself rarely drank.

Oona died relatively young, at sixty-six. To avoid another bizarre gravesite happening, she had ordered her coffin cocooned in cement when it was interred in the Vevey cemetery.

It was only death that at last freed Chaplin from his lifelong fear of a pratfall back into poverty and a horror of following his mother into fits of insanity.

He had shown impeccable timing, in the manner of Shakespeare or Newton, to be born at just the right time to exercise his genius. If the glover's son from Stratford-upon-Avon were alive today, he'd be writing screenplays while producers carped that his stories were too talky, advising him to seek other employment. And if Isaac Newton had been born during the centuries before apples were cultivated in England, how would he have discovered gravity?

Chaplin, the supreme pantomime artist, turned up exactly at the right moment, as movies were going through their silent, pantomime epoch. Had he shuffled to Hollywood a couple of decades later, the playful Great God Charlie would be unknown.

He was a deity trying to conceal his feet of clay—his mortal passions for the spotlight and for uncommon day labor. As his son and namesake noticed, "He might be late for other appointments or social engagements, but he was never late to work." He was a deity who punched a time card.

No mortal had held in his comic grasp so many diverse people of the earth. Einstein adored the Little Tramp, and so did every chimney sweep. The cowboy wit and movie star Will Rogers famously noted that "the Zulus know Chaplin better than Arkansas knows Garbo." He was referring to the fabled star of movies, both silent and sound: Greta Garbo.

"In any thousand years, only a few legendary men like Chaplin appear to beguile us," noted a contemporary writer. To which Laurence Olivier, a screen legend himself, brashly added, "He was perhaps the greatest actor of all time."

The decades and generations are hard on celebrity. Even kings and queens, once great, are forgotten. And today's audiences demand movies in color. Nevertheless, Chaplin, almost entirely in black-and-white, survives. In an auction a decade after his death, his cane and battered derby hat sold for more than $151,000. No clown, no entertainer, has had more books written about him than little Charlie Chaplin, shuffling along from nickel comedian to golden immortal.

At almost any hour of the day or night, someone, somewhere, is watching an old movie of the Little Tramp, and laughing to wake the dead.

Exit, smiling, Sir Charlie.

A CHARLIE CHAPLIN TIME LINE

1885 Chaplin's older brother, Sydney, born, March 16.

1889 Charles Spencer Chaplin born, April 16, in Walworth, South London, above his grandfather's cobbler's shop. During World War II, the house was destroyed by bombs.

1892 Chaplin's half-brother Wheeler Dryden born, August 31; soon vanishes.

1895 Hannah Chaplin hospitalized for first time with a touch of madness.

1896 Charles and Sydney confined to workhouse. Soon the brothers are transferred to the Hanwell Schools for Orphans and Destitute Children.

1898 Charles's father arrested for failure to support his sons. All year, both boys in and out of workhouse and schools for the poor. December, Charles gets job clog dancing with stage troop, the Eight Lancaster Lads.

1901 At age thirty-seven, the senior Charles Chaplin dies.

1903 Chaplin, the boy actor, begins touring in Sherlock Holmes play.

1905 Hannah Chaplin committed to asylum for the insane. Remains there for the next seven years.

1908 Charlie begins performing with one of Fred Karno's vaudeville acts.

1910 The Karno troupe lands in New York. Chaplin steals the show with his top-hatted drunk act.

1913 Signs to act in comedies for Keystone Film Company at $150 per week. He won't return to England for ten years.

1914 Makes thirty-five silent films at breakneck pace in one year.

1915 Begins writing, acting in, and directing his movies for Essanay, a Chicago production company, at approximately ten times the salary. He made a mere fourteen films that year, including his burlesque of the opera *Carmen*.

1916 Already the most popular actor in the world, he agrees to make his movies for Mutual Film Corporation at $10,000 a week plus a bonus of $150,000.

1917 Shoots one of his enduring films, *The Immigrant.* Signs a contract with a new company, First National, for a salary of more than $1 million. Late in the year, Chaplin begins construction of his own state-of-the-art studio in Hollywood. It's still there.

1918 Goes on war-bond tour with Douglas Fairbanks and Mary Pickford. Shoots his war comedy, *Shoulder Arms.* Great success. Marries Mildred Harris. Great failure.

1919 Joins a few Hollywood heavy-hitters to form United Artists, in order to become independent of rapacious film companies. Shoots the first of his feature-length masterpieces, *The Kid.*

1920 Chaplin is divorced from Mildred Harris.

1921 Hannah Chaplin, health improved, travels to Hollywood. Heading the other way, Chaplin returns in triumph to England and Europe.

1924 Begins shooting the second of his most celebrated films, *The Gold Rush.* Marries Lita Grey.

1926 Shoots his comic extravaganza *The Circus.* Despite the clowns, the lion, and escaped monkeys, it's pure, distilled Chaplin.

1928 Hannah Chaplin dies. Lita Grey divorces Charlie.

1931 *City Lights* premieres, to great acclaim. Chaplin begins world tour.

1934   Commences shooting *Modern Times* with Paulette Goddard.

1936   The last of the great silents, *Modern Times*, is released. Charlie and Goddard sail for the Far East and marry there.

1938   The first of Chaplin's talkies, *The Great Dictator*, begins shooting. War in Europe.

1940   World premiere of *The Great Dictator*. Cheers, mostly. Hitler didn't like it.

1942   Chaplin and Goddard divorce. Joan Barry breaks into his house.

1943   Barry accuses Chaplin of being father of her unborn child. He marries Oona O'Neill.

1944   Blood tests prove Chaplin could not be father of Joan Barry's child. He loses in court anyway.

1947   *Monsieur Verdoux*, a comedy of murder, opens. Mixed reviews. Chaplin's liberal politics get caught up in communist witch hunts. First shouts for him to be deported.

1952   Finishes shooting *Limelight*, the last film he will make in his own studio. Sails with family for Europe; his permission to return to the U.S. is scrapped.

1953   Chaplin and family buy estate in Switzerland, where he will remain for the last twenty-five years of his life.

1957   Directs himself in his final leading role as *A King in New York.* The film was a miss in a long, creative career.

1964   Publishes his autobiography.

1965   Death of his brother Sydney.

1967   Chaplin boldly tries, at age seventy-seven, to make a last film, *A Countess from Hong Kong,* his first in color. At best, a curiosity.

1972   On a ten-day pass from U.S. Immigration, Chaplin returns to Hollywood in April to receive a Special Academy Award.

1975   On a more leisurely trip to London, Chaplin is knighted by Queen Elizabeth II. He is now Sir Charles.

1977   Dies in his sleep, at home, in Vevey, Switzerland, on Christmas Day.

1978   His body is dug up and held for ransom, March 1. Two weeks later, it is recovered. The body snatchers are convicted months later.

Closely united in their early Cockney life together, the three Chaplins ended their saga strewn about the world: Hannah in Hollywood; Sydney and Sir Charlie in Switzerland.

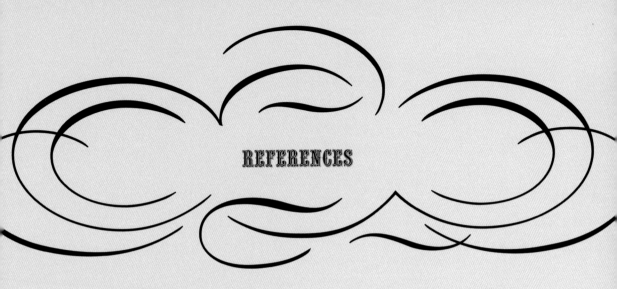

REFERENCES

Here's the evidence for all quotes. In addition, to avoid interrupting the flow of the narrative while identifying secondary celebrities, I am making fuller introductions here.

It's here, too, that I have exiled casual comments, some of them diverting.

ABBREVIATIONS

Auto	*My Autobiography*, Charles Chaplin
Hayes	*Charlie Chaplin: Interviews*, Kevin J. Hayes, ed.
Huff	*Charlie Chaplin*, Theodore Huff
Lynn	*Charlie Chaplin and His Times*, Kenneth S. Lynn
Junior	*My Father, Charlie Chaplin*, Charles Chaplin, Jr.
McCabe	*Charlie Chaplin*, John McCabe
McCaffrey	*Focus on Chaplin*, Donald W. McCaffrey, editor
McDonald	*The Films of Charlie Chaplin*, Gerald D. McDonald, Michael Conway, and Mark Ricci
Mitchell	*The Chaplin Encyclopedia*, Glenn Mitchell
Moss	*Charlie Chaplin*, Robert F. Moss

Opinion	*Chaplin: The Mirror of Opinion*, David Robinson
Norman	*What Happens Next: A History of American Screenwriting*, Marc Norman
Payne	*A Biography of the Tramp Played by Charles Chaplin*, Robert Payne
Reeves	*The Intimate Charlie Chaplin*, May Reeves and Claire Goll
Schickel	*The Essential Chaplin*, Richard Schickel, ed.
Trip	*My Trip Abroad*, Charles Chaplin
von Ulm	*Charlie Chaplin, King of Tragedy*, Gerith von Ulm
Robinson	*Chaplin: His Life and Art*, David Robinson

INTRODUCTION, OR LADIES WILL PLEASE REMOVE THEIR HATS

Page

2   a keen observer of Cockney life . . .

It was said that you were a Cockney if you lived within the sound of Bow bells, which were rung from a church in the City of London. The residents, from laborers to fishmongers to pickpockets, spoke a slang of their own with an uneducated accent consigning them to the social basement. The street swells among them sometimes dressed in clothing sewn with thousands of pearl buttons flashing like lightning bugs. With the growing din of the big city, the sound of Bow bells doesn't carry as once it did, and the number of Cockney citizens may have shrunk. Charlie Chaplin escaped the sound of his birthright by retuning his consonants and vowels.

2   "Sore feet . . . from whom I learned to walk." Moss, p. 18.

2   the shambling walk strolled him into immortality.

The splayed walk was partly achieved by wearing the big shoes on the wrong feet.

3   "that whirling gust of joy . . ." Payne, p. vii.

3   Impersonators shuffle along the sidewalks . . . .

    As often as not, two or more "Chaplins" shuffle around competing for sidewalk tips.

4   the theater manager shoved Charlie onto the stage . . . Auto, p. 20–21.

    One yearns for the Chaplin commentators to agree on the story details. A biographer claims that it was his father who shoved Charlie on stage: an absurdity, as the senior Chaplin had long before deserted the family. A second says Hannah herself did the shoving. Not likely. I have stuck with Chaplin's own memory of the teapot mystery. The theater manager, he says, done it. At this late date, no one cares, but the ink-stained biographer is obliged to get the details right.

4   "That night was my first appearance on the stage . . ." Ibid., p. 21.

4   "the funniest man in the world." Mitchell, p. 105.

CHAPTER 1: THE BOY IN THE BLUE VELVET SUIT

10   " . . . she could sit upon." Auto, p. 14.

11   "I was hardly aware of a father." Ibid., p. 18.

12   a squalid basement room . . .

    Chaplin would use the setting many times in his films and almost exactly in *Easy Street*, his comic homage to street life so tough that the police enter the neighborhood only with stretchers, to reclaim fallen comrades.

CHAPTER 2: BLEAK HOUSES

13   Charlie carried a chair on his back . . . Reeves, p. 96.

    A scene so visual and arresting, one wonders if it isn't the second cousin to Chaplin's classic end scene of the forlorn tramp setting off along a deserted road to an uncertain future.

14 "She gave the most luminous . . . I wanted to die that very night . . ." Auto, p. 24–25.

15 "Like sand in an hourglass . . ." Ibid., p. 27.

15 "We existed in a cheerless twilight." Ibid., p. 22.

15 she was discovered wrapping single lumps of coal . . .

Gifts of coal were not entirely mad. It was a tradition among the Scottish and others to offer the lumps of fuel on New Year's Eve, with the saying, "Long may your chimney smoke." Even in the U.S., at Christmastime, a piece of coal used to be threatened as a stocking gift to a child who had been bad.

Chapter 3: Life in the Booby Hatch

17 "owing to the absence of their father and the destitution and illness of their mother . . ." Robinson, p. 19.

19 "sadness." Auto, p. 28.

21 But he also grew chain mail on his skinny boy's armor.

The family clung to the belief that the Chaplin name descended from French Huguenot ancestors in an anglicized form, referring to the *chapeline*, the mailed hood in body armor.

21 "baffling despair . . ." Auto, p. 34.

21–22 "Why had she done this . . . how could she go insane?" Auto, p. 34.

Chapter 4: Life With Father

23 "Everything looked as sad as Louise . . ." Auto, p. 35.

24 "You'll sleep where you're told to," Ibid., p. 35.

25 "I had never seen a lopsided drunk before," Ibid., p. 38.

25 "Where the hell . . . She won't let me in," Entire dialogue exchange, Ibid., p. 38–39.

Chapter 5: Poster Boy

29 "They're going to kill it!" Auto, p. 41.

30 " . . . against being short-changed." Ibid., p. 41.

31 "Eight perfectly drilled lads . . ." *The Magnet*, July 14, 1900; cited in Robinson, p. 28.

31 " . . . almost fall asleep on the stage." *Winnipeg Tribune*, November 29, 1912; cited in Robinson, p. 34.

32 "The last thing I dreamed of was becoming a comedian . . . ." McCabe, p. 15.

34 There was standing room only. Opinion, Robinson, p. 3.

Chaplin's memory of his father's grandiose funeral and burial appear to have been a wishful fantasy. Records show that the senior Chaplin was thrown into a pauper's grave.

34–35 "The women always responded: 'Who is it, son?' And I would lower my voice . . ." Auto, p. 60.

Chapter 6: On Becoming Invisible

36 "I would steal out in the early morning . . ." Auto, p. 72.

38 "Mother went insane." Ibid., p. 74.

38 "If only you had given me a cup of tea . . ." Ibid., p. 75.   .

Chapter 7: Enter, Sherlock Holmes

39 If Charlie had heard of Faust . . .

Faust is a quirky character in a classic novel by the German author Johann Wolfgang von Goethe. The hero has done his bargaining in stage dramas, in great operas by Gounod and Berlioz and in the movies. Mephistopheles, who held Faust's pawn ticket on the future, would have been surprised.

40 "I realized I had crossed . . . I wanted to weep." Auto, p. 78.

41 "Don't lose your way . . ." Ibid., p. 81.

CHAPTER 8: DON'T MUG TOO MUCH

42 "I mugged too much when I talked." Auto, p. 78.

43 "He certainly is a tiny man." Lynn, p. 73.

43 "It was a depressing comedown," Auto, p. 88.

44 "At that time Jewish comedians were all the rage . . ." Ibid., p. 96.

44 "Within a year I might rise . . ." Ibid., p. 96.

45 "I don't have that honor." Documentary film: *Charlie Chaplin, The Forgotten Years.*

CHAPTER 9: A RED NOSE

46 "I had already discovered the secret of being funny . . ." McCabe, p. 25.

47 Almost every movement he made . . . was Chaplinesque. See him shuffling cards, in *The Immigrant*; counting bills, *Monsieur Verdoux.*

48 "We wanted to slough our skins . . ." Auto, p. 85.

48 "He appeared stand-offish . . . ." Robinson, p. 78.

48 "He didn't teach Charlie and me . . . He just taught us most of it." Lynn, p. 87.

50–51 "I understand you did poor business . . . Maybe he stinks, but . . ." Entire dialogue exchange, Auto, p. 117.

51 "This is it!" Ibid., p. 121.

53 "Good morning, Hudson . . . . I dreamt I was being chased by a caterpillar." Entire dialogue exchange, Ibid., p. 122.

CHAPTER 10: THE TIPSY GENTLMAN

57 Charlie was earning $75 a week. Auto, p. 124.
    Seventy-five dollars a week to the modern reader will seem a pittance, but almost a hundred years of inflation

converts the figure into at least fifteen or twenty times that amount. For comparison, Charlie later reports checking into New York's elegant Hotel Astor. It was $4.50 a night.

57 His other reading fed a deeper need.
Chaplin recalled reading but not finishing them all.

59 "I was impressed . . . a little fellow who could move like a ballet dancer . . . ." McCabe, p. 43.

60 "Is there a man named Chaffin in your company . . ."
Auto, p. 137.

Chapter 12: The Galloping Tintypes

63 "I thought you were a much older man . . . . I can make up as old as you like." Auto, p. 140.

65 "a wilderness of 'sets . . .'" McCaffrey, p. 30.

66 "comedy is an excuse for a chase . . ." Auto, p. 147.

66 Keystone provided no scripts.
"We have no scenario," Chaplin quotes Mack Sennett, in the comedian's *My Autobiography*, page 141. Evidently Sennett didn't want his story men to squander Keystone time and money writing in complete sentences.

66 Sennett would verbally fling forth a bare-bones storyline . . .
Norman, p. 57.
Sennett's gag men were supposed to recite the plot in thin air for him to pass along. But, and behold! Chaplin, writing in an earlier autobiography, *Charlie Chaplin's Own Story*, Bobbs-Merrill, Indianapolis, 1916, cited in McCaffrey's *Focus on Chaplin*, p. 31, describes a director with a cigar in one hand and manuscript in the other. Was it the racing form?

67 "People don't come to the movies to read . . . ."
Norman, p. 37.

67 "This was . . . antagonism with Lehrman." Auto, p. 143.

68 "I wanted everything a contradiction . . . I assumed the character and strutted about . . ." Ibid., p. 144.

68 "Even the clown has his rational moments." Trip, p. 1.

68 "A tramp, a gentleman, a poet, a dreamer, a lonely fellow . . ." Auto, p. 144.

70 "His club consists of the sidewalk . . ." von Ulm, p. 68.

CHAPTER 13: THE LENS LOUSE

72 The sequence is believed to have taken a mere forty-five minutes to shoot . . . . McDonald, p. 27.

Chaplin would make another half-reel film, a gem often overlooked as a trifle. In *The Professor*, he plays a dispirited, whip-cracking master of trained fleas who shuffles into a flophouse for a night's sleep. The performing vermin escape, of course. It's seven or eight minutes of pure character and exquisite pantomime. Failing to find a place for the cameo, Chaplin reprised the same act in *Limelight*, but it lost a little.

CHAPTER 14: MABEL, THE MOVIE STAR

73 "I've been in this business over ten years . . . ." Auto, p. 148.

74 "the specter of nervous breakdown . . ." Trip, p. 3.

75 "We have no time! . . . Miss Normand, I will not do what I'm told. . . ." Auto, p. 149.

77 "Do what you're told or get out." Ibid., p. 149.

CHAPTER 15: OPUS ONE: THE SLEEPWALKER

79 . . . a maximum thousand-dollar budget. Auto p. 158.

On a later film, *Dough and Dynamite*, Chaplin ran over

budget $800. He had to forfeit his bonus of $25 for writing and directing. The picture went on to gross more than $130,000 in its first year.

80 "a park, a policeman, and a pretty girl." Documentary film: *The Life and Art of Charles Chaplin.*

82 "The Spearmint Movement,—Very Wrigley . . ." Keystone Film, *Caught in a Cabaret*, 1914.

82 "He wanted to work—and nearly all the time. . . ." Lynn, p. 125, citing a Sennett letter to the American novelist Theodore Dreiser.

83 "It is pure instinct with me . . ." Quoted in Hayes, p. 84.

84 "There was a lot Keystone taught me . . ." Auto, p. 152.

85 As an actor he had to learn not to look at the camera.

Chaplin was not a genius of consistency. Sometimes on a reaction take or shot, he'd gaze directly into the camera. While he swore off the primitive humor of the pie in the face, as noted elsewhere, he clung to the primitive pratfall into the tub of water.

85 "I was entering a rich unexplored field . . . ." Auto, p. 152.

CHAPTER 16: CHARLIE AND THE TEN-GRAND RUMOR

86 It was called *Tillie's Punctured Romance* . . .

Chaplin costarred with stout Marie Dressler, a Canadian-born Broadway musical comedy sensation who went on to a long and beloved movie career. She won an Academy Award in 1930.

It was in *Tillie's Punctured Romance* that the director, Mack Sennett, may have inadvertently invented Hollywood's enduring "cute meet," when a couple bound for romance first meet in an amusing way. Here, Tillie throws a rock for her dog to fetch, misses the family cur, and hits the approaching stranger, Charlie, as a scheming fortune hunter. He, too, is a cur.

87 "But *I* don't make that." Auto, p. 159.

87 Along came a cowboy star, Broncho Billy . . .

Behind the cameras, Broncho Billy was Gilbert Anderson, privately Max Aronson. Essanay was a rendering of the producers' initials, S and A. Anderson/Aronson. Broncho Billy acted in *The Great Train Robbery*, the first smash-hit movie. He would make each of his Westerns in a day, claimed Chaplin, retreading seven sagebrush plots, and making millions of dollars in the saddle.

89 "The deal's on . . ." Auto, p. 160.

90 "like playing cards every Monday morning." Ibid., p. 166.

The young woman was Louella Parsons, who left for California and became as famous as any of the stars she wrote about in her newspaper movie columns—and infinitely more powerful. When she coughed in print, the box office wiped its nose. Production studios genuflected as if she were a goddess with a double chin.

90 "I don't use other people's scripts . . ." Ibid., p. 165.

90 She claimed later that she acted like a wooden board on purpose . . . Robinson, p. 136.

One of Gloria Swanson's greatest hits came late in life when she played the broadly satirical, aging, self-consumed actress in Billy Wilder's 1950 classic *Sunset Boulevard*.

92 "a wizened little man . . ." *Opinion*, Robinson, p. 135.

Turpin, penurious in his private life, bought an apartment house after he became rich and famous as a Keystone comedian. Before catching the nickel streetcar to work in the mornings, he'd sweep out the place instead of hiring a janitor.

He regarded his crossed eyes as his meal ticket and insured them from ever uncrossing with Lloyd's of London for $25,000. Since he was a devout Catholic, coworkers would alarm him when claiming they were praying nights that his eyes would straighten out. (*Wikipedia.*)

92 A $10 bet was put up . . .

In *Trilby*, a sensational novel of the late nineteenth century by George du Maurier, the evil Svengali uses hypnotism to gain control of the beautiful aspiring opera singer Trilby. The tale has been made into a film many times, but never before with cross-eyed Ben Turpin as the hypnotist.

92 Though he hated to write letters . . .

Chaplin's personal correspondence could be filed in a pay envelope. From the time Chaplin arrived in the States, twenty-two months passed before he sent off a letter to Sydney and inquired after their mother.

CHAPTER 17: CHARLIE AND THE CROSS-EYED MAN

98 Only Charlie could cut, add to, or alter his films.

Rarely even today are film directors given command over their movies. They are routinely awarded "first cut," entitling them to be first in the cutting room. After that, the production company may go at the film with a meat ax.

100 "HE'S HERE!" Auto, p. 177.

CHAPTER 18: THE MILLIONAIRE TRAMP

108 there he impaled his splayed footprints . . .

In the matter of setting footprints in permanent cement, he anticipated by ten years the famous forecourt at Grauman's

Chinese Theatre in Hollywood. He left his footprints there as well, but the cement proved to be fly-by-night. During the communist witch-hunting panics of the 1950s, with the mindless drop in Chaplin's popularity, the footprints disappeared. Charlie's old friend Sid Grauman, evidently showing no loyalty, ran for cover, jackhammer in hand.

108   The studio still stands . . .

The studio eventually passed into other hands and shrank from its original five acres to somewhat more than two. The film and television comedian Red Skelton briefly owned the studio, followed by CBS and A&M Records. Currently it is owned by the Jim Henson Company, giving command of the entrance to a statue of Kermit the Frog. The amphibian is costumed as the Little Tramp.

CHAPTER 19: DAWN ON SUNSET BOULEVARD

112   the picture segues into a mongrel Rin-Tin-Tin epic
with laughs.

Rin-Tin-Tin was a canine film star of the 1920s. He was a German shepherd capable of great strides and leaps, to the sorrow of assorted villains. He was credited with saving Warner Bros. from the quicksand of debt and bankruptcy. A barking clone came around for later generations under the name of Lassie.

112   "The cinema's first total work of art." Robinson, p. 229.
So declared Louis Delluc, a screenwriter of the 1920s.

CHAPTER 20: A MARRIAGE OF MAYFLIES

121   "Never," he replied emphatically. Huff, p. 89.

122   "I had been caught in the mesh . . . Although I was not

in love . . ." Auto, p. 230.

122 "It was cluttered with pink-ribboned foolishness . . . ."
Ibid., p. 239.

122 "as thrilling as winning . . . dazzlement." Ibid., p. 230.

Chapter 21: Where's Charlie?

127–28 The kid would . . . earn more than all his Irish ancestors
combined . . .

Coogan's mother and stepfather, on drugs, blew his movie
earnings, reckoned at $4 million. As a result, California
passed new legislation to protect a child's earnings from
predatory parents. It's called Coogan's Law. It came too late
to do Jackie much good. He grew to be six feet tall and an
adult actor. He may be remembered as the bald Uncle Fester
in the grave-happy TV series *The Addams Family*.

128 " . . . a royal court headed by an absolute monarch."
Lynn, p. 198.

128 "rude, untutored genius . . ." Lynn, p. 218.

128 "Even in slapstick, there is an art." Huff, p. 120.

Chapter 22: Room Service

133 Second Thoughts Consider Will Be Best . . .
Robinson, p. 262.

133 " . . . she couldn't extract a penny from him with a vacuum
cleaner . . ." Mitchell, p. 126.

135 Mildred settled for $200,000 . . . *New York Times*, Nov. 13,
1920

Chapter 23: The Eternal Washtub

136 "Yes . . . and you are Jesus Christ." Auto, p. 252.

138 "a little old lady." Ibid., p. 254.

138 "If only . . . think of the thousands of souls you could have saved." Ibid., p. 287.

138 "I have a notion that he suffers from a nostalgia for the slums." Ibid., p. 270.

139 "In my pursuit of bread and cheese . . ." Ibid., p. 257.

Chapter 24: Déjà Woes

143 Chaplin boils a hobnailed boot . . .
Charlie's prop can be traced back to his cobbler grandfather.

143 Meanwhile, he chews down the shoelaces . . .
  The boot and laces were made of licorice, a mild laxative. After so many retakes, the licorice stopped production by putting the two actors to bed for a couple of days.

146 Her speech was burdened with a light lisp . . .
  Georgia Hale's movie career ended with the arrival of sound pictures. She became a Los Angeles dance instructor. Like almost everyone who came in contact with Chaplin for longer than twenty minutes, she wrote a memoir of the events. She died in 1985.

148 "You knew you were working with a genius." Robinson, p. 352.

Chapter 25: Dancing Around the Stake

149 "Chaplin is a genius!" McDonald, p. 184.

150 "It was the torture of complete incompatibility." Junior, p. 32.

150 "stout yellow house on the hill . . ." Ibid., p. 37.

153 "The very morons who worshipped Charlie Chaplin six weeks ago . . ." Lynn, p. 311.

CHAPTER 26: SILENCE SPOKEN HERE

154 "... charming." Documentary film: *Charlie Chaplin, The Forgotten Years.*

157 In October 1927, Warner Brothers released a modified musical ...

Al Jolson was a vaudeville singing star whose popularity almost topped Chaplin's. His footlight charisma was high voltage. After inaugurating sound with *The Jazz Singer,* he made several more movies, of modest success.

157 "They are ... ruining the great beauty of silence." Lynn, p. 321.

159 It was as if their past together had forged itself to a festering memory.

He could hardly have dispelled the memory of being totally abandoned during his poorhouse years, when Hannah disappeared for more than a year. Interested scholars, Charlie himself among them, have been unable to trace his mother's faded footprints during that vanishing act.

CHAPTER 27: THE IMPERTINENT GESTURE

163 "Everything I do is a dance." Robinson, p. 399.

165 "a film is like a tree ..." Ibid., p. 395.

166 "It is a mistake to dally long in the public's adulation ...." Auto, p. 382.

CHAPTER 28: FIVE FRANCS A GLANCE

167 "The world was an entertainment ..." Auto, p. 337.

168 " the dead returning ... I was almost physically sick with emotion." Robinson, p. 425, citing Thomas Burke's "A Comedian."

169 "I can't understand all this stuff . . . ." "What Made Charlie Run," *Los Angeles Times*, April 16, 1989.

CHAPTER 29: THE RED FLAG

178 "I am not a communist agitator . . . ." Documentary film: *Charlie Chaplin, The Forgotten Years.*

CHAPTER 30: WELCOME TO TOMANIA

179 "This was unthinkable . . . ." Auto, p. 366.

179 . . . the same absurd stub of a black mustache. McCabe, p. 190. Hitler's mustache. The biographer claims that it was widely believed in Berlin, early in Hitler's career, that he clipped his handlebar for a comic rendering in imitation of Chaplin. This, to enhance his acceptance by the wild popularity of the Little Tramp in Germany. Hardly persuasive. Hitler would certainly have shaved off the thing, since he believed that Chaplin and his mustache were Jewish.

182 "Syd and I lost our hearts to Paulette at once . . . ." Junior, p. 150, following photo section.

182 a shooting script of immense length . . . Robinson, p. 493.

CHAPTER 31: THE PHANTOM JEW

185 "This little Jewish tumbler . . ." McCabe, p. 190. Tumbler = acrobat.

185 "You must be Spanish," I tell her. Entire dialogue exchange, Trip, p. 146.

186 "I'm the logical choice . . . ." McCabe, p. 8.

186 Was he a descendant, through his father, of French Jews? Huff, p. 11.

187 "he had lost faith in the romantic stories . . ." Lynn, p. 68.

188 "I don't have that honor." Documentary film: *The Art and Life of Charlie Chaplin.*

188 "of Jewish extraction." McCabe, p. 198, citing Chaplin to a reporter from *McClure's Magazine,* 1916.

One may dismiss as a curiosity how comfortable Chaplin felt in tight company with Jews, not excepting his brother Sydney. His closest friend was the smiling, irrepressible Douglas Fairbanks, whose father was Jewish. So, too, was Paulette Goddard's father. Claire Bloom, his leading lady in *Limelight*—Jewish. Even his pard, Broncho Billy, the film cowboy, from the old days, spoke Yiddish.

It's a curiosity that in his 1919 silent film *Sunnyside,* it amused him to make his heroine, Edna Purviance, Jewish. A quick shot of her father reveals him reading a Yiddish newspaper.

190 "To gauge the morals of our family by commonplace standards . . ." Auto, p. 19.

CHAPTER 32:   THE COCKNEY CAD

192 "a savage comic commentary . . ." McDonald, p. 209–10.

192 She eventually married a famous novelist . . .

Goddard's fourth and last husband was Erich Maria Remarque, a German anti-Nazi, whose novel *All Quiet on the Western Front* remains the classic of the First World War. Goddard died in Switzerland at age seventy-nine, leaving an estate of $20 million.

195 "A Cockney cad!" McCabe, p. 207.

CHAPTER 33:   THROW THE RASCAL OUT!

198 "The banality of evil." From Hannah Arendt, *Eichmann in*

Jerusalem: A Report on the Banality of Evil. New York, NY: Penguin, 1994.

199 " . . . people come to see me." Lynn, p. 449.

201 Called the House Un-American Activities Committee . . .

One member of the committee was so carried away by the hunt that he enquired whether Christopher Marlowe was a communist. The famous sixteenth-century playwright refused to answer.

201 "Proceed with the butchery." Lynn, p. 463.

202 "I am not a Communist!" Op. cit.

CHAPTER 34: SO LONG, CHARLIE

205 "This was not the day . . . It was the day of politics." Robinson, p. 573.

CHAPTER 35: TAKES AND MISTAKES

211 His younger half-brother, Wheeler Dryden, left behind in Hollywood . . .

Wheeler's son, Spencer Dryden, wandered into the spotlight as drummer for Jefferson Airplane, a hugely successful rock group in the 1960s and 70s.

213 "will take me at least another year to finish . . ." Junior, p. 367.

213 The result was a polished manuscript . . .

Charles Chaplin Jr. would write a memoir of his own; see the Bibliography. He acted in several of his father's films, including *Limelight*. The junior Charles died relatively young in 1968. His brother, Sydney, who became a Tony Award–winning stage actor, lived on in California until 2009. Their mother, Lita Grey, clung to her distant fame until 1995. She, too, wrote a book about Chaplin.

214–15 "The past isn't dead. It's not even past." From *Requiem for a Nun*, Faulkner, William, NY, Random House, 1951.

CHAPTER 36: BRIMSTONE IN THE AIR

217 "A fearsomely cruel man." Lynn, p. 16.

217 "The saddest thing I can imagine . . ." Auto, p. 337.

217 "The public liked *A Countess from Hong Kong* . . ." Mitchell, p. 75.

218 "taking the nap . . ." Auto, p. 102.

CHAPTER 38: A LIFE IN CONCRETE

227 "disturbing the peace of the dead." Robinson, p. 631.
Wardas, the younger man, evidently regarded as the brains of the scheme, was imprisoned for four-and-a-half years. The bewildered Bulgarian, Ganev, got a break; he was punished with a mere suspended sentence.

229 "He might be late . . . but he was never late to work." Junior, p. 111.

229 "the Zulus know Chaplin . . ." Quoted in Schickel, p. 122.

229 "In any thousand years, only a few legendary men like Chaplin . . ." Payne, p. 286.

229 " . . . the greatest actor of all time." Robinson, p. 631.

PHOTOGRAPH AND ILLUSTRATION SOURCES

Chaplin Archives
pp. 20, 28, 49, 52, 138, 144 (top), 158, 194, 208. Photos ©
from the Chaplin archives.

Roy Export SAS
pp. 93, 132, 144 (bottom), 145, 147, 151 (bottom), 155, 162,
171, 173, 175, 183, 197. Photos © Roy Export SAS.

Jeffrey Vance Collection
pp. 27, 69 (right), 111, 114, 117, 125, 189 (both), 231. Photos
courtesy of the Jeffrey Vance Collection.

Susan Chick
pp. 64 (bottom), 107 (both), 151 (top), 206 (top), 212, 219.
Photos courtesy of Susan Chick.

Kobal Collection
pp. 16, 76, 200. Photos courtesy of The Kobal Collection.

Brown Brothers
pp. 120, 206 (bottom). Photos courtesy of Brown Brothers.

United Press International
pp. 225, 226. "Charlie Chaplin's Body Stolen" and "Chaplin's Remains Found, Pair Held." © 1978 United Press International, Inc. All rights reserved.

John Cannon Collection
p. 69 (left). Photo courtesy of the John Cannon Collection.

Bison Archives
p. 64 (top). Photo courtesy of the Bison Archives.

Library of Congress
p. 56. "Sir Charles Chaplin, 1889–1977, full-length portrait, seated, facing right; playing cello." December 13, 1915.

Other Sources
p. 222. Illustration from *My Trip Abroad*, by Charlie Chaplin. Harper & Brothers, 1922.

pp. 88. Sheet music cover from author's personal collection.

pp. i, 9, 81, 96, 105, 116, 126. Photos from author's personal collection, courtesy of the Academy of Motion Picture Arts and Sciences.

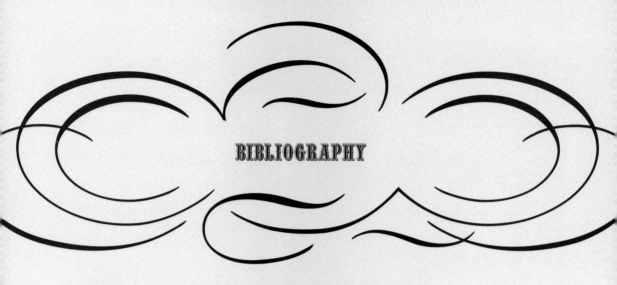

BIBLIOGRAPHY

BOOKS ON CHARLIE CHAPLIN ABOUND. HERE ARE THE titles I found most useful in rendering him for a last curtain call. I have chosen to sidestep the alphabet by listing my sources in the order of their grandeur.

Chaplin, Charles. *My Autobiography*. New York: Simon and Schuster, 1964.
Chaplin had a gripping rags-to-riches story to tell. He eschewed ghosts and wrote it himself. More restrained than most autobiographers in improving on reality, he nevertheless cheated the truth now and then.

Robinson, David. *Chaplin: His Life and Art*. New York: McGraw-Hill, 1985.
Chaplin has been fortunate in his biographers. Robinson is his Boswell. Not only does Robinson write with charm, he allows no Chaplin detail to escape without researching it back through the mists. Contains filmography. The Olympian among biographies.

Lynn, Kenneth S. *Charlie Chaplin and His Times*. New York: Simon and Schuster, 1997.
Second only to Robinson. A gem, nevertheless. Added attention paid to the times and world around Chaplin. My copy well flagged with Post-its.

Chaplin, Charles Jr. *My Father, Charlie Chaplin*. New York, Random House: 1960.
A third-dimensional view. Both devotional and critical.

Von Ulm, Gerth. *Charlie Chaplin, the King of Tragedy*. Caldwell, Idaho: The Caxton
Printers, 1940.

Mitchell, Glenn. *The Chaplin Encyclopedia*. London: B.T. Batsford, 1997.
Invaluable, especially for checking out name spellings and other obscurities.
Some text material not found elsewhere.

McCabe, John. *Charlie Chaplin*. Garden City, NY: Doubleday, 1978.
Contemporary in time, following Chaplin's death in 1977. Useful on the
Jewish question, a subject dodged by some biographers.

Huff, Theodore. *Charlie Chaplin*. New York: Arno Press, 1972.
Brief biography, followed by detailed story descriptions of Chaplin's
major films, ending with *Monsieur Verdoux*.

McDonald, Gerald D. and Michael Conway and Mark Ricci. *The Films of
Charlie Chaplin*. New York: Citadel, 1965.
One of many filmographies, going back to Chaplin's first movies.

Gehring, Wes D. *Charlie Chaplin: A Bio-Bibliography*. Westport, Connecticut:
Greenwood Press, 1983.
A patchwork, with one article attributing Chaplin's character and even his
violin playing to Gypsy blood. Useful appendixes.

Schickel, Richard, editor. *The Essential Chaplin*. Chicago: Ivan R. Dee, 2006.
The latest collection of articles about Chaplin.

Chaplin, Charles, *My Trip Abroad*. New York: Harper & Brothers, 1922.

Robinson, David. *Chaplin: The Mirror of Opinion*. Bloomington, Indiana:
Indiana University Press, 1984.

An assortment of articles by many hands, some by Chaplin himself. Contains filmography.

McCaffrey, Donald W., editor. *Focus on Chaplin*. Englewood Cliffs, New Jersey: Prentice-Hall, 1971.
A collection valuable for its lingering over Chaplin's working methods.

Hayes, Kevin J., editor. *Charlie Chaplin: Interviews*. Jackson, Mississippi: University Press of Mississippi, 2005.

Moss, Robert F. *Charlie Chaplin*. New York: Pyramid, 1975.

Payne, Robert. *Great God Pan: A Biography of the Tramp Played by Charles Chaplin*. New York: Hermitage House, 1952.
Rhapsodic.

Reeves, May and Claire Goll. *The Intimate Charlie Chaplin*. Jefferson, North Carolina: McFarland, 2001.

Norman, Marc. *What Happens Next: A History of American Screenwriting*. New York: Harmony Books, 2007.

DOCUMENTARIES

Charlie Chaplin, The Forgotten Years. Universal City: Hart Sharp Video, 2003.

Schickel, Richard, director. *The Art and Life of Charles Chaplin*. Los Angeles: Lorac Productions, 2003.

The Unknown Chaplin. London: Thames Television, 1982.

A SELECTION OF CHAPLIN FILMS

CHARLIE CHAPLIN APPEARED BEFORE THE CAMERA FOR the first time in 1914. He went on to make short films at a frenetic pace, sometimes as often as two a week. Many in this vast treasury of one- and two-reelers are only of scholarly interest.

For the profoundly smitten, complete filmographies are available in both Robinson volumes listed in the bibliography. In addition the reader will find there books that are expanded filmographies, such as *The Films of Charlie Chaplin.*

I have made a selection, from the miles of film, of those in which I feel that Chaplin put his best footage forward.

Kid Auto Races at Venice. Keystone Comedy, 1914.
The Little Tramp makes his debut.

Mabel's Strange Predicament. Keystone Comedy, 1914.
Charlie gets his hand caught in a spittoon.

His Favorite Pastime. Keystone Comedy, 1914.
Charlie doing his drunk impersonation.

Caught in the Rain. Keystone Comedy, 1914.
Funny!

Laughing Gas. Keystone Comedy, 1914.
Charlie as dentist's assistant with a mallet. You can imagine . . .

Tillie's Punctured Romance. Keystone Feature, 1914.
First full-length comedy feature, based on a stage play. Charlie plays a charming scoundrel. A major hit.

His New Job. Essanay Comedy, 1915.
Charlie and the cross-eyed Ben Turpin compete for a job. Great physical comedy.

A Night Out. Essanay Comedy, 1915.
Charlie and Ben Turpin again, almost upstaged by a flying custard pie. First screen appearance of Edna Purviance.

In the Park. Essanay Comedy, 1915.
Classic park comedy.

The Tramp. Essanay Comedy, 1915.
Chaplin introduces pathos to the comedy form.

The Floorwalker. Mutual Comedy, 1916.
Chaplin discovers a new comedy prop—the escalator.

The Vagabond. Mutual Comedy, 1916.
Funny, funny washtub scene.

The Pawnshop. Mutual Comedy, 1916.
Famous stethoscopes-applied-to-alarm-clock comedy bit.

The Rink. Mutual Comedy, 1916.
Charlie, fabulous on skates.

Easy Street. Mutual Comedy, 1917.
Charlie as a cop. A masterpiece of mayhem.

Shoulder Arms. First National, 1918.
Charlie as a foot soldier. Laughter in the trenches. Who knew?

The Kid. First National, 1921.
A masterpiece.

The Gold Rush. United Artists, 1924.
Another masterpiece.

The Circus. United Artists, 1928.
Abounds with Chaplin's unique comedy inventions. Don't miss this one.

City Lights. United Artists, 1931.
A gem.

Modern Times. United Artists, 1936.
Classic.

The Great Dictator. United Artists, 1940.
Genius.

Monsieur Verdoux. United Artists, 1947.
Genius's day off.

Limelight. United Artists, 1952.
Chaplin puts strokes of autobiography on film.

While Chaplin made a few more films, it was clear that after *Limelight* he had outlived his genius.

INDEX